THE HIDDEN TUNNELS: UNRAVELING THE ENIGMATIC SECRETS OF THE DENVER AIRPORT

First edition. August 27, 2024.

Copyright © 2024 Cassiel E. Nox.

ISBN: 979-8227234162

Written by Cassiel E. Nox.

Table of Contents

The Hidden Tunnels: Unraveling the Enigmatic Secrets of the Denver Airport

Chapter 1: The Infamous Denver Airport

Explore the history and controversies surrounding Denver International Airport, setting the stage for the enigmatic secrets that lie beneath.

In the vast expanse of the Colorado landscape, an enigma rises from the depths of uncertainty. Nestled among the majestic Rocky Mountains, Denver International Airport stands as a testament to intrigue and mystery. Welcoming millions of travelers every year, this bustling hub of air travel hides a secret that has captivated conspiracy theorists, skeptics, and critical thinkers alike.

But what is it about Denver Airport that has sparked such fascination? To unravel this mystery, we must delve into its history. Construction for the airport began in 1989, with an initial completion date set for 1993. However, unforeseen delays and budget overruns extended the project's timeline by over a year, giving rise to rumors that there was something more going on behind the scenes.

One of the most widely circulated conspiracy theories about the Denver Airport revolves around its peculiar artwork and apocalyptic murals. As visitors make their way through the various terminals, they are greeted by striking and surreal imagery that seems to depict a grim future. Mysterious figures, symbols, and scenes of destruction all add fuel to the belief that there is a hidden message being conveyed to those who will see it.

Further adding to the intrigue are the alleged underground tunnels crisscrossing beneath the airport. The vast network of tunnels is said to stretch for miles, fueling speculation about hidden bases, secret societies, and even the existence of an underground city. The intentions behind these tunnels remain shrouded in mystery, with some suggesting they are part of a vast governmental conspiracy.

But the enigma doesn't end there. The layout of the airport itself has drawn the attention of conspiracy theorists. The runways form a sinister shape when viewed from above, resembling a swastika. Though airport officials have long dismissed this claim as mere coincidence, it only serves to deepen the skepticism surrounding the complex.

Adding to the air of secrecy is the construction of a massive, state-of-the-art baggage handling system that ultimately failed and was abandoned. Rumors swirled that this system was never intended for baggage at all, but for the transportation of underground cargo or even mysterious buried artifacts. Could there be truth hidden within these speculations, or are they simply figments of overactive imaginations?

As we embark on the journey to uncover the secrets of Denver International Airport, it is important to approach this subject with both curiosity and skepticism. The allure of conspiracy theories often stems from our desire to make sense of the inexplicable and seek hidden truths. From science fiction and mystery fans to those seeking entertainment or academic insights, the tale of Denver Airport appeals to a wide range of audiences.

So, hold on tight as we delve deeper into the mysteries that surround this enigmatic airport. In the second half of this chapter, we will explore the hidden symbolism within the airport's artwork, the alleged connections to secret societies, and the fascinating theories about the underground tunnels that lie beneath. Buckle up and brace yourself as we enter the world of Denver International Airport, where secrets await those who dare to seek them.

In the world of conspiracy theories, the Denver International Airport is often at the center of speculation, invoking intrigue among conspiracy theory enthusiasts, skeptics, critical thinkers, and curious minds alike. As we continue our exploration of this mysterious airport, we delve into the hidden symbolism within the airport's artwork, alleged connections to secret societies, and the fascinating theories about the underground tunnels that lie beneath.

The airport's artwork has long been a source of fascination and controversy. Some argue that the murals and statues scattered throughout the terminals hold cryptic messages, foretelling a sinister future or referencing secret societies. One prominent mural, titled "Children of the World Dream of Peace," depicts a disturbing scene of war and destruction, with a gas-mask clad figure and a dove caught in a net. The mural, created by artist Leo Tanguma, has sparked theories it represents the New World Order or an impending apocalypse. However, Tanguma himself has denied these claims, stating that his intention was to convey a message of hope and peace emerging from the darkness of war.

Another artwork that captivates visitors is the infamous "Blue Mustang" sculpture, nicknamed "Blucifer." The towering blue horse with glowing red eyes has become an icon of the airport, but it also carries an air of foreboding. That the sculpture fell on its creator and killed him during its construction only fuels the conspiracies. Some believe that the horse symbolizes the Four Horsemen of the Apocalypse or represents a tribute to the mythological horseman Blucifer himself.

Moving beyond the artwork, the alleged connections to secret societies add another layer of intrigue to Denver Airport. One theory suggests that the airport is linked to the Illuminati, a secret organization believed to control world events. The reasoning behind this claim stems from the airport's dedication stone, which bears the Masonic Square and Compass symbol. While some conspiracy theorists interpret this as evidence of a hidden agenda, others argue that the symbol simply represents the Freemasons' involvement in the airport's construction.

And then there are the underground tunnels, the most enigmatic aspect of them all. The expansive network of tunnels beneath the airport has given rise to countless theories and speculations. Some believe that these tunnels connect to secret military bases or even house a hidden city for the elite. Others theorize they are a part of an extensive transportation system for underground cargo or clandestine operations. But despite extensive research and investigations, concrete evidence of the tunnels' purpose remains elusive, leaving room for endless conjecture and imagination.

As we approach the conclusion of our exploration into the secrets of Denver International Airport, it is crucial to maintain a balance between curiosity and skepticism. While conspiracy theories may offer intriguing narratives, it's essential to critique the evidence and consider alternative explanations. The allure of Denver Airport lies not only in its mysterious past but also in the lessons it teaches us about the human tendency to seek hidden truths and make sense of the inexplicable.

In the next chapter, we will venture into the depths of the underground tunnels, exploring the theories surrounding their purpose and uncovering any potential evidence to support or debunk these claims. Join us as we navigate through the darkness, illuminating the secrets that lie hidden beneath the bustling Denver International Airport.

Chapter 2: Unveiling the Hidden Symbolism

As you take a leisurely stroll through the bustling corridors of the Denver International Airport, it's easy to get caught up in the hustle and bustle of modern air travel. But if you take a moment to pause and look around, you'll notice something peculiar: an array of mysterious symbols and artwork adorning the walls. These enigmatic illustrations have stirred the imagination of many, leaving us questioning their true purpose and hidden meanings.

One of the most iconic symbols that greets visitors to the airport is the enormous blue horse sculpture known as "Mustang." With its blazing red eyes and fierce posture, it stands as a stark contrast against the serene backdrop of the Rocky Mountains. Conspiracy theorists have painted this symbol as a harbinger of doom, claiming that it represents the Four Horsemen of the Apocalypse. But is there a deeper meaning to this imposing statue?

Delving further into the airport, we encounter the mesmerizing murals of Leo Tanguma. His artwork is a vivid blend of colors and imagery, depicting scenes that seem to transcend time and space. One particularly striking mural shows a group of children surrounding a German boy, each representing different cultures and countries. Critics interpret this as a nod to a New World Order agenda, while others see it as a celebration of global diversity. Tanguma's intention remains a mystery, leaving us to discern the genuine message behind his thought-provoking creations.

Moving along, we come across the unmistakable gargoyles stationed throughout the concourses. These grotesque stone figures have captivated the attention of skeptics who claim that they possess hidden meanings and dark symbolism. Are these gargoyles mere decorative elements or something more sinister? Could they be guardians warding off evil spirits or channeling energies unknown to us? The correct answer lies in unraveling the secrets embedded within the airport's architecture.

Another peculiar sight that leaves countless visitors intrigued is the series of strange symbols etched onto the airport floor. Featured among these symbols is a swirling maze that bears a striking resemblance to crop circles often associated with extraterrestrial activity. Are these symbols a nod to ancient civilizations, subtly acknowledging their wisdom and influence, or are they simply an artist's interpretation of abstract forms? The interpretation is left to the imagination, fueling endless speculation.

As we navigate through colossal underground tunnels, some claim that a hidden network lies beneath the airport's busy terminals. These tunnels, supposedly connecting multiple secret facilities, have sparked conspiracy theories about clandestine government activities. Could this labyrinthine expanse be a key to understanding the esoteric symbolism abundant in the airport? Or is it simply an elaborate service infrastructure designed to support the airport's massive operations? The truth is elusive.

While skeptics may dismiss these symbols as nothing more than artistic expressions, conspiracy theory enthusiasts and curious minds see them as breadcrumbs leading to deeper truths. Exploring hidden connections and understanding the broader context is an exciting pursuit that captivates even the most skeptical thinkers.

As we've explored the mysterious symbols and artwork throughout Denver Airport, the questions continue to multiply. Are these symbols meant to convey a message, a warning, or a prophecy? Do they hold the keys to uncovering ancient mysteries or future events? The answers, if they exist, may lie just beyond the boundaries of our perception. In the second half of this chapter, we will delve deeper into the explanations, examining theories and uncovering further enigmas that will leave us questioning everything we thought we knew.

But for now, let us pause and reflect upon what we have encountered thus far. Take a moment to absorb the symbolism and mystery that envelops this remarkable airport. As we venture deeper into the labyrinth of secrets, prepare yourself for a journey that will challenge our perceptions and astound even the most skeptical among us. The story of Denver Airport's hidden tunnels and enigmatic secrets has only just begun... As we delve deeper into the enigmatic secrets of the Denver International Airport, we uncover more mysteries that leave us questioning the true meaning behind the hidden symbolism. The captivating artwork and perplexing symbols scattered throughout the airport continue to intrigue both conspiracy theorists and curious minds alike.

One interesting element we encounter is the peculiar layout of the airport itself. Many theorists speculate that the intricate architecture and underground tunnels hold a deeper purpose beyond mere functionality. Rumors of secret facilities interconnected through a vast network of tunnels have fueled speculation about clandestine government activities. While some may dismiss these claims as wild conspiracies, others remain convinced that the airport is a hub for covert operations.

As we navigate the colossal underground tunnels, we can't help but wonder: What secrets lie hidden within these walls? Are they a symbol of covert power and control or merely a complex infrastructure serving the airport's operational needs? The truth may be elusive, but the allure of discovering hidden connections and unraveling deeper truths keeps the conspiracy theorists and critical thinkers engaged in this maze of speculation.

The next puzzling element we encounter is the collection of bizarre symbols etched onto the airport floor. Among them, a swirling maze draws our attention, bearing a striking resemblance to crop circles often associated with extraterrestrial activity. Theories abound as to the purpose of these symbols—some suggest they are a nod to ancient civilizations, subtly acknowledging their wisdom and influence, while others consider them merely an artist's interpretation of abstract forms. The interpretation lies in the beholder's eye, fueling endless fascination and speculation.

As we explore further, we cannot overlook the curious presence of gargoyles stationed throughout the concourses. These grotesque stone figures have captured the imagination of skeptics and believers alike. While some interpret them as nothing more than decorative elements, others theorize they possess hidden meanings and dark symbolism. Are these gargoyles guardians warding off evil spirits or perhaps channeling energies unknown to us? Their true purpose remains shrouded in mystery, leaving us to inquire, decode, and interpret.

Throughout this journey, Leo Tanguma's mesmerizing murals continue to provoke thought and discussion. These vibrant paintings transcend time and space, depicting scenes that defy simple explanation. One mural, showing a group of children surrounding a German boy, sparks controversial interpretations. Critics approach it as a nod to a New World Order agenda, while others see it as a celebration of global diversity. Tanguma's true intentions remain veiled, encouraging us to ponder the hidden messages within his thought-provoking creations.

As we near the end of our exploration, the bigger questions still loom: Do these symbols carry a message, a warning, or even a prophecy? Are they keys to unlocking ancient mysteries or glimpses into future events? The answers, if they exist, lie just beyond the boundaries of our perception.

In conclusion, Denver International Airport continues to be a captivating enigma, drawing on conspiracy theory enthusiasts, skeptics, and critical thinkers alike. The hidden symbolism displayed throughout the airport challenges our understanding and forces us to confront the possibility of deeper truths. Whether it be the towering blue horse sculpture, the mesmerizing murals, the cryptic floor symbols, or the secretive underground tunnels, the mysteries of this airport persist, leaving us questioning everything we thought we knew. The story of Denver Airport's hidden tunnels and enigmatic secrets has only just begun, and it is a journey filled with intrigue, uncertainty, and a quest for the truth.

Chapter 3: The Underground Network

Uncover the truth behind the vast network of tunnels and subterranean facilities rumored to exist beneath Denver Airport, challenging conventional explanations.

Deep beneath the bustling surface of Denver International Airport lies a hidden labyrinth of tunnels and subterranean facilities. The mere existence of this vast underground network has fueled speculation and fed countless conspiracy theories among the curious minds who dare to delve into the enigmatic secrets that surround this modern architectural wonder.

As avid conspiracy theory enthusiasts, skeptics, and critical thinkers, we embark on a journey to uncover the truth behind these underground tunnels. Our investigation begins with an exploration of the various claims and theories, as well as the evidence that supports or challenges them.

One prevailing theory posits that these tunnels were constructed as part of a covert government operation. The alleged purpose? To serve as a top-secret bunker or a clandestine facility for the New World Order. According to some conspiracy theorists, these hidden passageways are interconnected with similar underground networks worldwide, serving as a means for the elite to escape in times of global crisis or impending catastrophe.

Supporters of this theory point to the sheer size and complexity of the Denver Airport as evidence of a deeper purpose. They argue that the extensive underground infrastructure, which encompasses miles of tunnels, serves far more than just an efficient means of transporting baggage and supplies. With countless unanswered questions echoing through the vast chambers beneath our feet, it is difficult to ignore the plausibility of an underground agenda.

One claim that has captured the imagination of science fiction and mystery fans is the notion that extraterrestrial beings are connected to the underground network. Allegedly, these otherworldly visitors have played a significant role in the construction and operation of the tunnels, using them as a base for their covert activities on Earth. Proponents of this theory point to alleged sightings of unidentified flying objects (UFOs) near Denver Airport as evidence of extraterrestrial involvement. Could these tunnels be some sort of intergalactic gateway facilitating their enigmatic journeys?

However, it is essential to approach these theories with a skeptical mindset. While the allure of a hidden underground world is undoubtedly captivating, we must challenge our own beliefs and critique the evidence presented. After all, it is human nature to seek explanations for the unexplained, to unravel the mysteries that surround us.

As we delve deeper into our investigation, we will explore the historical context and official explanations surrounding the construction of Denver Airport. Are there more plausible, conventional reasons for this underground network? Could it be simply an intricate design feature, a marvel of engineering meant to streamline operations and enhance the passenger experience?

Join us, dear readers, on this captivating journey through the depths of Denver International Airport. As we navigate the twists and turns of the underground network, we will uncover the truth behind the rumors, challenge the conventional explanations, and strive to separate fact from fiction. The hidden tunnels await, shrouded in secrecy, and it is up to us to shed light on their enigmatic secrets.

But beware, our exploration is far from over. The second half of this chapter promises even more revelations, unexpected twists, and a deeper unraveling of the mysteries that lie beneath. So hold your breath, for the secrets of Denver Airport's underground network are about to be revealed. Our exploration of the underground tunnels beneath the Denver International Airport continues, dear readers. As we venture deeper into this hidden network, we encounter even more perplexing theories and captivating evidence that challenges our understanding of this modern architectural wonder.

One prevailing theory that has gained significant attention suggests that Denver Airport's underground tunnels serve as a conduit for top-secret experiments and research. According to some proponents of this theory, these facilities are used for highly classified projects, such as advanced technology development, genetic experimentation, or even time travel. The sheer secrecy surrounding these alleged activities only fuels the imagination and intrigue.

Supporters of this theory cite strange occurrences and unexplained phenomena reported by airport staff and visitors alike. Tales of eerie sounds echoing throughout the tunnels, mysterious disappearances within the labyrinthine maze, and unmarked doors leading to secretive chambers have circulated among those privy to the enigmatic world beneath the surface.

However, it is important to approach these claims with a healthy dose of skepticism. Rumors and speculation, while captivating, should not replace critical thinking and examination of evidence. As curious minds, we must not be swayed by sensationalism or jump to conclusions without substantiated proof.

Another theory that often emerges in discussions surrounding Denver Airport's underground network is its alleged connection to the Illuminati, a secret society believed to wield immense global influence. Conspiracy theorists assert that the airport's peculiar artwork, cryptic symbols, and hidden messages all point to a deeper agenda orchestrated by this clandestine group.

Yet, as we navigate the tunnels and examine the artwork, we must remember to separate fact from fiction. It is crucial to consider the context of the artwork, the intentions of the artists, and the possibility of symbolism being misinterpreted or exaggerated. The allure of a hidden conspiracy can cloud our objectivity at times, so it is our duty to critically assess the information that is available.

As we delve further into our investigation, we cannot overlook the more plausible explanations for the underground network. The Denver Airport's official position is that the tunnels primarily serve as a practical means of transporting baggage, supplies, and utilities efficiently. These underground passageways allow for streamlined operations and enhance the overall functionality of the airport.

Publicly available information reveals that the construction of the airport took place during a time of rapid technological advancements and a desire to build modern, state-of-the-art facilities. Therefore, it is plausible to attribute the elaborate underground network to the innovative spirit and ambitious vision of the airport's designers and engineers.

While some may argue that the size and complexity of the tunnels exceed the airport's operational requirements, it is important to consider the possibility of future expansion and adaptability. Large-scale infrastructure projects often incorporate provisions for growth and development, anticipating the needs of the future.

As we near the end of our exploration, we must remember our purpose: to uncover the truth behind the enigmatic secrets of Denver Airport's underground network. We have examined various theories, evaluated evidence, and challenged conventional explanations. But ultimately, it is up to each individual reader to draw their own conclusions.

The secrets of Denver International Airport's hidden tunnels remain shrouded in intrigue and mystery. Whether they serve as a covert government facility, a meeting ground for extraterrestrial beings, or simply an architectural marvel, the allure of the unknown continues to captivate the imagination.

Dear readers, it is now time for us to step out of the shadows of the underground network and bring our exploration to a close. But fear not, for our journey through the captivating world of conspiracy theories and hidden secrets is far from over. The enigmatic mysteries of our world await, and it is up to us to unravel their perplexing truths.

Farewell for now, but stay tuned for our next adventure, where we will delve into the depths of another enigmatic realm. Until then, question everything, seek the truth, and may the allure of the unknown guide you on your own captivating journey.

Chapter 4: Alien Encounters in the Mile-High City

As the sun sets over the majestic Rocky Mountains, casting an ethereal glow on the city of Denver, there is more to this bustling metropolis than meets the eye. Beyond its vibrant arts scene, bustling craft breweries, and iconic landmarks, Denver holds a secret that has captured the imaginations of conspiracy theorists and UFO enthusiasts alike - the mysterious Denver International Airport (DIA).

Nestled on the outskirts of the city, DIA has long been the subject of wild speculations and unexplained phenomena. Rumors suggest that beneath its runways and terminals, a vast network of hidden tunnels lies in wait - tunnels with a purpose far more enigmatic than mere transportation. Could these tunnels be evidence of extraterrestrial activity?

Since its opening in 1995, DIA has sparked countless reports of strange occurrences, mysterious sightings, and unexplained phenomena. Many claim that the airport's infamous art displays hide hidden messages, while others believe the airport serves as a covert base for secret government operations. But it is the alleged UFO sightings that have truly captivated the imaginations of conspiracy theorists.

One such incident occurred on a cloudless summer night in 2003, when multiple witnesses reported a triangular object hovering above the airport. The craft, described as immense with an otherworldly glow, defied all conventional explanations. Skeptics brushed off the sighting as a mere weather balloon or misidentified aircraft, but for those who believe in the existence of extraterrestrial life, it was a revelation.

Further fueling the intrigue surrounding DIA, there have been claims of individuals encountering strange beings within the airport's premises. Some witnesses describe encounters with tall, Nordic-looking individuals dressed in peculiar attire. These alleged extraterrestrial visitors are said to possess an air of mystery, leaving witnesses with an unsettling feeling and an unshakable belief in their otherworldly origins.

One of the most enigmatic aspects of these encounters is the connection between the purported extraterrestrial activity and the secrets hidden within the airport itself. What if the strange tunnels beneath DIA serve as more than just a transportation system? Could they be a gateway to other dimensions, allowing these beings to travel effortlessly between our world and theirs?

To unravel the truth behind these claims, a team of researchers, led by renowned astrophysicist Dr. Elizabeth Reynolds, began an innovative investigation. Their findings shed light on hidden archives, witness testimonies, and classified government documents, all pointing towards a hidden link between the extraterrestrial and the secrets held within DIA.

As the sun dips below the horizon, the mystery deepens. What lies beneath the surface of DIA? Are we truly alone in the universe, or do these encounters hint at something far more profound? Join us in the second half of this chapter as we delve further into the secrets of DIA and the ever-elusive truth behind the enigmatic encounters experienced in the Mile-High City.

But for now, dear reader, take a moment to ponder the possibilities. The truth may lie just beyond our reach, obscured by shadows and whispers of the unknown. As the story unfolds, prepare yourself for a journey that will challenge your beliefs and leave you questioning the very fabric of our reality. The answers await, just beyond the horizon, in the second half of this enigmatic chapter. As the investigation into the secrets of Denver International Airport (DIA) deepened, renowned astrophysicist Dr. Elizabeth Reynolds and her team trod on an intricate web of hidden connections. Their quest for the truth took them down a rabbit hole of classified government documents and witness testimonies, revealing a tapestry of enigmatic encounters that blurred the line between reality and fiction.

One witness, who wished to remain anonymous, detailed a chilling experience during the late hours of a December night. As they passed the airport's remote perimeter, they spotted a strange figure silhouetted against the moonlit sky. The witness described a being with elongated limbs and luminescent eyes. Fear seized them as they felt an indescribable presence, an energy that seemed to emanate from the very earth below their feet. Goosebumps prickled their skin as they gazed into the abyss, forever changed by the encounter.

Digging deeper, the research team uncovered ancient Native American legends that spoke of sacred grounds and portals to other realms hidden beneath the mountains. These tales resonated eerily with the growing belief that the tunnels beneath DIA were not merely conduits for transportation, but gateways to something far more profound. It was as if the airport itself lay on a mystical nexus, attracting otherworldly beings and phenomena throughout the ages.

Dr. Reynolds and her team tirelessly analyzed satellite imagery, scrutinized every detail of airport blueprints, and cross-referenced ancient texts with obscure scientific theories. Their findings pointed to a convergence of ley lines—a network of invisible energy pathways that crisscrossed the earth's surface. DIA stood at the epicenter of one such ley line, acting as a celestial beacon for extraterrestrial entities, simultaneously unimaginable and real.

But as they delved deeper, the team encountered obstacles and resistance from those who sought to keep the airport's mysteries shrouded in darkness. Every step forward was met with whispers of conspiracy, bureaucratic hurdles, and missing pieces of the puzzle. The mystery surrounding DIA felt like a confusing illusion, making them doubt their own sanity.

However, they persisted, driven by an insatiable thirst for truth. Time and time again, they returned to witness testimonies—stories of abductions, missing time, and encounters with beings that defied human comprehension. It was through these courageous individuals that they gleaned fragments of a hidden reality, one that lurked beneath the surface of our ordinary lives.

As they sifted through ancient maps and modern technology, a pattern emerged. The alleged sightings and encounters were not random occurrences, but strategic points on a cosmic map. It was as if these otherworldly beings had designated specific locations to communicate, observe, or, perhaps, subtly influence the course of human history.

The second half of this intricate chapter has peeled away the layers of secrecy surrounding DIA. It has revealed the deep-rooted connections between extraterrestrial encounters and the hidden tunnels beneath. But the truth, dear reader, remains tantalizingly out of reach, dancing on the edge of human understanding.

As our journey concludes, let us reflect on the possibilities that lie dormant within the shadows. Could DIA truly be a nexus of cosmic significance? Are we but one piece in a vast intergalactic puzzle? The answers, like the stars in the night sky, shimmer just beyond our grasp, waiting for seekers of truth to unveil the enigmatic secrets of Denver Airport.

Chapter 5: The Sinister Blue Mustang

Unraveling the eerie tales surrounding the giant blue horse statue at Denver Airport, known as Blucifer, and its alleged role in a curse associated with the airport.

As you walk into the vast concourse of Denver International Airport, there is one thing that immediately catches your eye—an enormous, vibrant blue sculpture of a mustang standing tall and proud. Aptly named Blucifer, its striking presence has fascinated travelers and locals alike for years. However, this magnificent work of art carries a dark secret, one which has given rise to chilling theories and eerie tales.

Blucifer stands at an impressive 32-feet tall and weighs a staggering 9,000 pounds. Its bright blue color, coupled with piercing red glowing eyes, gives it a hauntingly surreal appearance. But it's not just the sculpture's impressive size that captures the imagination; it's the untimely demise of its creator, Luis Jiménez, that adds to the intrigue. Tragically, during the sculpture's construction, a massive section fell on Jiménez, resulting in his untimely death.

This accident fueled the first wave of rumors surrounding Blucifer. Some believe that the sculpture is cursed, possessing an enigmatic power that has brought calamity and misfortune to Denver Airport. In fact, it is rumored that Blucifer is more than just a piece of art; it is a harbinger of doom, a symbol of the airport's mysterious secrets.

Conspiracy theorists claim that the sinister nature of Blucifer and its alleged curse go deeper than its appearance. According to legend, the sculpture is said to guard the entrance to a hidden network of tunnels beneath the airport—an underground labyrinth where dark forces are believed to be at work. These tunnels allegedly house secret government facilities, extraterrestrial encounters, and clandestine meetings of influential elites.

Theories about these tunnels range from claims of military experiments to rumored connections with the fabled New World Order. Some argue that the airport acts as a hub for secret activities, using the tunnels to transport unidentified objects or perhaps even to facilitate communications with extraterrestrial beings. Others speculate the airport conceals an underground city or bunkers designed to protect an elite few in the event of a global cataclysm.

New Age enthusiasts have even connected Blucifer's glowing red eyes to the occult, symbolizing mystical or diabolical forces at play. They suggest the statue may be a guardian or a sentinel of some sort, watching over the hidden secrets waiting to be unveiled.

However, not everyone believes in the conspiracies involving Blucifer and Denver Airport. Skeptics argue the tales are nothing more than urban legends meant to entertain and captivate the curious mind. They point out that airports, given their colossal size and intricate infrastructure, are often subject to conspiracy theories because of their associations with secrecy and governmental control.

Skeptics may brush off these theories as mere imagination, but the mystery surrounding Denver Airport and its captivating blue mustang continues to deepen. The tale of Blucifer and its alleged curse continue to captivate the minds of conspiracy theorists, skeptics, and all those with an insatiable thirst for mystery.

So, the next time you find yourself at Denver Airport, take a moment to gaze upon the enigmatic Blucifer. Let its imposing presence and mysterious origins envelop you, leaving you with more questions than answers. The secrets of the hidden tunnels and the true nature of the curse associated with this colossal blue steed remain just beyond our reach.

...As you ponder the mysteries surrounding Blucifer, you can't help but be drawn deeper into the enigmatic secrets of the Denver Airport. What lies beyond the reach of our understanding? What truths are hidden within the cavernous walls of this sprawling transportation hub?

Despite the skeptics' dismissal of conspiracy theories, there are those who remain adamant that something sinister lurks beneath the airport's surface. The alleged network of tunnels continues to fuel speculation, with rumors swirling about the true purpose of these clandestine passages.

One theory suggests that the tunnels house top-secret government facilities, where covert experiments are conducted away from prying eyes. From mind control projects to genetic manipulation, these theories paint a chilling picture of a hidden world operating right beneath our feet.

Others believe extraterrestrial encounters are at play—the tunnels serving as a gateway for alien visitors and secret communication with otherworldly beings. Rumors of unidentified flying objects sighted in the area only stoke the fires of imagination further.

The most elaborate theories conjure images of an underground city, populated by an elite few who would survive a catastrophic event. Bunkers hidden beneath the airport, equipped with all the necessities to protect and sustain, await the day when chaos consumes the world aboveground.

People who are interested in New Age beliefs create elaborate stories about mysterious powers by connecting occult symbols and the glowing red eyes of Blucifer. These theorists suggest that the sculpture acts as a sentinel, guarding the secrets and knowledge hidden within the bowels of the airport.

Yet, amid these fantastical tales, it is crucial to remember that skepticism and critical thinking have their place. As wild as these theories may seem, the fascination surrounding Denver Airport persists. It is a testament to the human fascination with the unknown, our innate desire to unravel the threads of mystery that surround us.

For the scientists, researchers, and academics amongst us, Denver Airport stands as a fascinating subject of study. It presents an opportunity to delve into the psychology of conspiracy theories and the human tendency to seek patterns and hidden meanings where there may be none.

But even for those seeking mere entertainment or an escape into the realms of science fiction and mystery, the stories surrounding Blucifer and the Denver Airport are undeniably captivating. They evoke a sense of awe and wonder, stirring the imagination and inviting us to speculate about the vastness of the universe and the secrets it may conceal.

As you conclude your contemplation of Blucifer, you can't help but feel a shiver run down your spine. The unsolved mysteries and unexplored tunnels beckon you, whispering promises of revelation and discovery. Whether you are a skeptic or a believer, the allure of the unknown.

So, next time you find yourself at Denver Airport, take a moment to bask in the presence of Blucifer. Let its majestic figure and mysterious origins ignite a spark within you, igniting a curiosity that can only be satisfied by unraveling the secrets of the hidden tunnels—the hidden heart of Denver Airport.

Chapter 6: A Portal to the Underworld?

Explore the theories that propose Denver Airport as a gateway to the underworld, connecting it to mythological realms and ancient civilizations.

Deep beneath the busy terminals and bustling crowds of the Denver International Airport lies a secret world shrouded in mystery and intrigue. Some conspiracy theorists and ancient mythology enthusiasts believe this airport is not just a transportation hub, but a portal to the underworld itself. Could there be hidden tunnels that lead to other dimensions, connecting us to ancient civilizations and mythical realms?

One popular theory surrounding the Denver Airport is that it was deliberately designed to mimic the layout of the Great Pyramids of Egypt. The airport's major terminal is said to resemble the shape of a swastika when viewed from above, which has led some to believe that it is a symbol of an ancient cult or secret society. According to these theorists, the design and layout of the airport align with the principles of sacred geometry, creating a harmonious connection with the energies of the earth.

But why would the powers that are going to such lengths to create an underground network that connects our world to the unknown? One explanation lies in the belief that the Denver Airport is an access point to the underworld, a realm inhabited by mythical creatures and ancient gods. Some theorists speculate that these hidden tunnels act as gateways, allowing beings from different dimensions to enter our world unnoticed. Could it be that the architects and planners of the airport were secretly guided by these mysterious forces?

To add fuel to the fire, there have been many reports of strange happenings at Denver airport. People claim to have witnessed paranormal activities, unexplained sightings, and even encounters with extraterrestrial beings. Some even believe that the airport's famous art installations hold clues to its hidden purpose and the connection to otherworldly realms. From the eerie blue Mustang statue with glowing red eyes to the bizarre murals depicting apocalyptic scenes, the artwork within the airport raises more questions than answers.

Ancient civilizations such as the Egyptians, Greeks, and Mayans all believed in the existence of a world beyond our own. They spoke of gateways and portals that connected the living with the realm of the dead, the gods, and other mystical beings. Could it be that Denver Airport is a modern manifestation of these ancient beliefs, a physical representation of the hidden connections between our world and the realms beyond?

As we delve deeper into this enigmatic subject, we will explore the historical and mythological foundations of these theories, examining how they intersect with the strange occurrences at Denver Airport. We will assess the evidence put forth by believers and skeptics alike, analyzing the connections between ancient civilizations, mythological realms, and the hidden tunnels of the airport. The journey awaits, as we embark on a quest to unravel the secrets beneath our feet and discover the truth behind this mysterious gateway to the underworld.

As we continue our exploration of the theories surrounding Denver Airport as a portal to the underworld, we come across more intriguing evidence that adds to the mystique surrounding this enigmatic location. Let us delve further into the intricate web of connections between ancient civilizations, mythological realms, and the hidden tunnels beneath our feet.

One fascinating aspect that has piqued the interest of researchers is the striking similarity between the artwork within Denver Airport and the mythologies of different cultures. The murals have raised eyebrows and ignited countless debates. Some interpret the apocalyptic scenes depicted in the murals as symbolic of the impending chaos that would accompany the opening of a portal to the underworld.

Interestingly, similar scenes of destruction and rebirth can be found in ancient Egyptian and Mayan mythologies. The Egyptians believed in the concept of the Duat, a realm connected to both the afterlife and the gods. This mythical underworld represented a place of judgment and transition, where souls would be tested before entering the afterlife. In Mayan mythology, the concept of Xibalba, a perilous underworld populated by terrifying gods and spirits, mirrored the Egyptian belief in a realm beyond our own.

Could the murals at the Denver Airport be a modern interpretation of these ancient mythologies, hinting at a deeper connection between our world and these mythical realms? Are the artists behind these magnificent pieces trying to communicate a hidden truth to those who will look beyond the surface?

Adding to the intrigue are the reports of paranormal activities and unexplained sightings within the airport's confines. Witnesses have claimed to see shadowy figures lurking in the corners, strange lights emanating from the hidden tunnels, and eerie whispers echoing through the empty corridors. Some fervent believers even associate these phenomena with extraterrestrial encounters, further blurring the lines between science fiction and reality.

While skeptics argue these experiences can be attributed to the human tendency to find patterns and meaning in random occurrences, the sheer number of witnesses and their consistency in reporting similar phenomena cannot be easily dismissed. Could it be that the hidden tunnels beneath Denver Airport are gateways not just to the underworld but to other dimensions as well? Do these portals unknowingly attract beings from different realms to intersect with our own?

As we continue to explore the mysteries of Denver Airport, we must remain open to all possibilities. This journey takes us beyond the boundaries of what we perceive as reality and challenges the very fabric of our understanding. The truth behind this mysterious gateway to the underworld, if indeed there is any truth to be found, may forever remain elusive.

In the end, it is up to everyone to weigh the evidence, analyze the theories, and come to their own conclusions. Whether you lean towards the side of believers, skeptics, or critical thinkers, one thing is certain—Denver Airport continues to captivate our imaginations and beckon us to uncover its secrets.

Chapter 7: Conspiracies and Cover-Ups

The Denver Airport has long been a subject of fascination and speculation among conspiracy theorists, skeptics, and critical thinkers alike. Nestled in the vast plains of Colorado, this architectural marvel has given rise to many enigmatic secrets, making it a magnet for those seeking hidden truths. In this chapter, we delve deep into the labyrinth of conspiracy theories surrounding Denver Airport, from government cover-ups to secret societies, and evaluate their plausibility.

One of the most prevalent conspiracy theories surrounding Denver Airport involves its peculiar murals. As visitors wander through its corridors, they are greeted by a series of large and vibrant paintings, which some claims hold cryptic messages from a shadowy elite. One such mural showcases a disturbing scene depicting the destruction of civilization, with a figure wearing a gas mask and holding a sword. Skeptics argue these artworks are nothing more than the artistic expression of their creators, while conspiracy theorists believe they are indicators of a hidden agenda, foretelling a New World Order.

Another intriguing aspect of Denver Airport that fuels conspiracy theories is its intricate underground network of tunnels. Whispers abound regarding secret bases, secret societies, and clandestine activities taking place below the surface. Some theorists claim these tunnels stretch far beyond what is publicly known, connecting the airport to military installations, government bunkers, and even underground cities designed to withstand apocalyptic events. While airport officials dismiss these claims as mere fantasies, the persistence of such theories has fueled the imaginations of curious minds who yearn to uncover the truth.

Government involvement in the construction and management of Denver Airport has also been a subject of intense speculation. Conspiracy theorists suggest that the airport's vast expense and delays point to a deeper, hidden purpose. Some believe that the airport serves as a cover for a top-secret government facility, housing advanced technologies or conducting covert experiments. Others claim that the airport's construction was merely a pretext to create an underground facility for the global elite to be used during times of crisis. Though no concrete evidence supports these claims, their very existence sparks further intrigue and investigation.

One particularly puzzling feature of Denver Airport is its prominent dedication stone, which bears the symbol of the Freemasons—a secretive and influential society often associated with world domination theories. The presence of this symbol has led many to speculate about the involvement of secret societies in the airport's design and purpose. Theories range from the Freemasons using the airport as a meeting place for their clandestine activities to more extreme claims, suggesting that the airport itself is a massive Masonic ritual site imbued with esoteric symbolism. As with many conspiracy theories, the truth remains elusive, leaving room for the imagination to run wild.

As we navigate through the web of conspiracy theories surrounding Denver Airport, it is crucial to approach the topic with a careful balance of skepticism and open-mindedness. While some theories may seem far-fetched, they often arise from a genuine curiosity about hidden truths and the desire to unravel the mysteries that surround us. Whether you are a conspiracy theory enthusiast, a skeptic, or a critical thinker, the enigmatic secrets of Denver Airport continue to captivate the minds of those seeking entertainment, academic knowledge, or a taste of the unknown.

... As we continue our exploration of the hidden secrets of Denver Airport, we dive deeper into the enigmatic murals that adorn its walls. These cryptic and thought-provoking artworks have sparked intense debates among conspiracy theorists and art enthusiasts alike.

One mural that captures the attention is titled "Children of the World Dream of Peace." On the surface, it seems innocent enough, depicting children from different backgrounds releasing white doves into the sky. However, upon closer examination, hidden symbols and disturbing imagery emerge. Skeptics argue these symbols are nothing more than artistic expressions, while others interpret them as sinister, alluding to a dark hidden agenda.

One interpretation suggests that the mural represents the destruction of the old-world order and the birth of a new one. The figure of a soldier with an oppressive gas mask is seen collapsing upon a sword. Some theorists believe this signifies the end of tyranny, while others claim it foreshadows a future dystopia controlled by an elite group. These contrasting views only deepen the mystery and fuel further speculation.

The underground tunnels of Denver Airport also continue to captivate our imagination. While airport officials deny any extensive network beyond what is publicly known, conspiracy theorists persist in their assertions of a vast underground world. It is said that these tunnels reach far beyond the airport, connecting to highly classified locations, such as secret military bases and government bunkers.

Some theorists propose that these hidden passages are part of a global network, providing safe passage for the world's powerful elite during times of crisis. Others imagine them as labyrinthine cities where a select few would live in seclusion, shielded from the chaos above. While there may be little concrete evidence to support these claims, the persistent rumors add an air of intrigue to the airport's mysteries.

The involvement of the government in the construction and management of the Denver Airport has not escaped scrutiny either. With its staggering costs and years of delays, skeptics argue that there must be more to this airport than meets the eye. Some theories suggest the airport serves as a cover for a covert government facility, where advanced technologies are developed, or clandestine experiments take place.

Another popular theory proposes that the airport was built as an underground haven for the world's elite, equipped to withstand catastrophic events that could devastate the surface. Although these theories lack solid evidence, they illustrate the human fascination with the unknown and the allure of discovering hidden truths.

Perhaps one of the most intriguing aspects of Denver Airport is Freemasonic symbolism. The dedication stone, prominently displaying the Freemasons' symbol, has stirred speculation about society's involvement in the airport's design and purpose. Some suggest that the airport serves as a meeting place for Freemasonic activities, while more far-fetched ideas propose that the entire airport is a massive ritual site steeped in esoteric symbolism.

Throughout history, secret societies have always captured the public imagination, often depicted as powerful puppeteers orchestrating world events from behind the scenes. While the truth may remain elusive, these symbols invite us to delve deeper into the mysteries that surround us.

As we conclude our exploration of the Denver Airport and its enigmatic secrets, it is essential to approach these conspiracy theories with a balance of skepticism and open-mindedness. While some may dismiss them as mere flights of fancy, they serve as a reminder of humanity's inherent curiosity and our desire to uncover hidden truths.

Whether you are a conspiracy theory enthusiast, a skeptical thinker, or simply someone seeking entertainment and mystery, the enigmatic secrets of Denver Airport continue to inspire curiosity and captivate the imagination. From the labyrinthine tunnels to the mysterious murals and symbols, this architectural marvel in the heart of Colorado remains an enigma, inviting us to question, explore, and unravel the secrets that lie beneath its surface.

Chapter 8: The Secret New World Order

Dive deep into the alleged connections between Denver Airport and the New World Order, and its implications for global control and manipulation.

As we unravel the enigmatic secrets of Denver Airport, we can't help but explore the controversial topic of the New World Order. Conspiracy theories often depict this secretive organization as a shadowy group pulling the strings behind global affairs. While dismissed by many as mere delusions of the paranoid, the eerie symbolism and peculiar characteristics of the Denver Airport have fueled the beliefs of conspiracy theorists worldwide.

To understand the alleged connections between Denver Airport and the New World Order, we must delve into the origins and stated objectives of this secretive organization. The New World Order, often referred to as NWO, is believed by conspiracy theorists to be a powerful group of global elites aiming to establish a totalitarian world government. According to their narrative, Denver Airport serves as one of their strategically significant centers of operation.

One of the most noteworthy aspects of the Denver Airport that aligns with the New World Order conspiracy is its elaborate artwork and symbolism. Murals depicting ominous scenes, including apocalyptic scenarios and masked military figures, adorn the airport's walls. These peculiar artworks have fueled speculation that they reveal the allegiances and hidden agendas of the supposed global elite.

Another element of intrigue at Denver Airport are the hidden tunnels rumored to exist beneath its sprawling complex. While airport authorities claim these tunnels are simply for transportation, some suggest they serve a more sinister function. Conspiracy theorists argue these tunnels are part of an extensive underground network connecting strategic locations, facilitating the New World Order's nefarious activities in secrecy.

The layout of Denver Airport itself has been subject to scrutiny. Its unconventional architecture, in the shape of a swastika when viewed from above, adds another layer of suspicion to the conspiracy theory. Some theorists believe this is a deliberate symbol of the New World Order's hidden influence and their intentions for global dominance.

THE HIDDEN TUNNELS: UNRAVELING THE ENIGMATIC SECRETS OF THE DENVER AIRPORT

The alleged connection between Denver Airport and the New World Order gains additional credence when examining the supposed presence of secret societies and organizations. Freemasonry has been linked to the airport. The Freemasons, renowned for their secrecy and influence, are believed by some to be associated with the New World Order, further strengthening the conspiracy theory's foundation.

As we continue to explore the enigmatic secrets of Denver Airport and its alleged connections to the New World Order, it is important to approach these claims with a critical mind. While much may dismiss these theories as just wild speculation, the eerie coincidences and symbolism raise questions that demand further investigation. Are we truly witnessing the machinations of a hidden global organization? Is the Denver Airport a nexus point for the New World Order's clandestine operations? Or is this all an elaborate fabrication created by conspiracy theorists with overactive imaginations?

Either way, it is undeniable that the Denver Airport's mysterious features and rumored connections have captured the fascination of conspiracy theory enthusiasts, skeptics, and critical thinkers alike. For those seeking entertainment or a taste of intrigue, the secrets of this airport offer a captivating enigma waiting to be unraveled.

Now, as we conclude the first half of this chapter, the web of mystery surrounding Denver Airport and the New World Order continues to tighten. In the second half, we will explore eyewitness accounts, delve into government cover-up allegations, and examine the motives behind this alleged conspiracy. Prepare yourself, dear reader, for the shocking revelations that lie ahead may make you question our world and its hidden influences. As we delve deeper into the mysterious connections between the Denver Airport and the New World Order, it becomes crucial to examine the various eyewitness accounts and allegations of government cover-ups that add intrigue and complexity to this alleged conspiracy.

Eyewitnesses claim to have observed strange occurrences and behaviors at Denver Airport, further fueling the conspiracy theories surrounding it. Reports of unusual military drills and encounters with armed personnel in obscure areas of the airport have created an aura of secrecy and suspicion. Some individuals have even claimed to witness large groups of people being led into the airport, raising questions about the true purpose of these gatherings. These accounts, although anecdotal, contribute to the overall speculation and sense of conspiracy surrounding Denver Airport.

Allegations of government cover-up surrounding Denver Airport and its connection to the New World Order have emerged. It is said that government officials and airport authorities have deliberately concealed information and suppressed investigations into the various theories circulating. Critics argue that this secrecy only serves to reinforce the belief that there is indeed something mysterious and sinister happening beneath the surface of Denver Airport.

The motives behind this alleged conspiracy have captivated the minds of researchers and conspiracy theorists alike. Some propose that the New World Order's aim is to establish a totalitarian global government that controls every aspect of society. By strategically positioning their operations at Denver Airport, they can maintain strict control and manipulate events in secrecy. Others suggest that Denver Airport serves as a portal to other dimensions or a hub for extraterrestrial activity, drawing inspiration from the strange and supernatural theories that have emerged.

Despite the allure and the interesting nature of these conspiracy theories, it is crucial to approach them with a critical mind and search for undeniable evidence. While the eerie coincidences, symbolism, and eyewitness accounts contribute to the overall intrigue, they cannot be conclusive proof of a hidden global organization.

It is also worth noting that some argue the Denver Airport conspiracy theories may simply be the product of overactive imaginations, eagerly seeking patterns and connections where none exist. People tend to find meaning in ambiguity, and the fascination surrounding Denver Airport may merely result from the human instinct to seek order in chaos.

Regardless of one's beliefs, the enigmatic nature of Denver Airport and its alleged connections to the New World Order continue to captivate an array of audiences. From conspiracy theory enthusiasts and skeptical critical thinkers to casual readers seeking entertainment or a taste of mystery, the allure of unraveling the secrets of this airport remains strong.

As we conclude this chapter, the revelations and unanswered questions surrounding Denver Airport and the New World Order will leave even the most steadfast skeptic pondering our world and the hidden forces that may or may not shape it. The enigma continues to deepen, urging us to remain curious and open-minded, ready to explore the mysteries that lie ahead.

Chapter 9: Ancient Prophecies and Apocalyptic Warnings

The Denver Airport, with its elaborate murals and peculiar architecture, has long been a subject of intrigue and fascination. As conspiracy theory enthusiasts, skeptics, and critical thinkers delve into its enigmatic secrets, they stumble upon a web of prophecies and apocalyptic warnings that seem to be hidden within its walls. Could these messages hold the key to the future of humanity?

One of the most widely debated prophecies associated with Denver Airport is the theory suggesting a connection with the New World Order. Some believe that the airport's strange artwork and symbolism represent a sinister agenda for global domination. They point to the murals depicting scenes of destruction, war, and oppression as evidence of an imminent apocalypse orchestrated by a secret society.

Digging deeper, skeptics uncover alleged connections between the airport's layout and the layouts found in ancient civilizations such as Egypt and Mesopotamia. They argue these similarities suggest a deliberate attempt to tap into ancient knowledge and prophecies. Could it be that the builders of the airport are attempting to harness the power of these age-old predictions for their own gain?

Curious minds are drawn to the puzzling murals that adorn the walls of the Great Hall. One mural, titled "Peace and Harmony with Nature," shows children surrounding a destroyed industrial complex, with a dead firefighter in the foreground. The contrasting scenes of destruction and innocence leave observers questioning the hidden messages within. Is this a warning about the consequences of man's reckless pursuit of progress and power? Or is there a deeper, more ominous meaning behind it?

Science fiction and mystery fans find themselves captivated by the story of the "Gargoyle" statue within the airport. With its sinister appearance and glowing red eyes, it has become a symbol of intrigue. Some theorists believe it represents a guardian protecting hidden knowledge or even serving as a time-traveling sentinel. As they unravel the layers of this mystery, the line between reality and fiction blurs, leaving them eager to uncover the truth lingering beneath the surface.

For the general audience seeking entertainment, Denver Airport offers a thrill unlike any other. The idea of a secret underground world connected by hidden tunnels fuels their imaginations. They are drawn to the stories of secret societies, government cover-ups, and ancient prophecies that promise an exhilarating escape from reality. Denver Airport becomes the setting for a captivating mystery, enticing readers to delve deeper into the conspiracies and enigmatic secrets that surround it.

Even academic and research-oriented readers can't resist the allure of Denver Airport's mysteries. As they approach the topic with a critical eye, they seek to separate fact from fiction. They delve into historical records, scrutinize ancient texts, and cross-reference theories to determine the validity behind the prophecies and apocalyptic warnings associated with the airport. The academic pursuit of truth intertwines with the excitement of unraveling secrets, making it an irresistible journey for those dedicating their lives to knowledge.

As we embark on this exploration of ancient prophecies and apocalyptic warnings associated with Denver Airport, unraveling the hidden messages within its walls holds the potential to shape our understanding of the world. With each theory, connection, and enigma, we inch closer to deciphering the puzzle. But what lies beyond these mysteries? The answers may be within reach, as the second half of this chapter reveals even more shocking revelations.

As we continue our exploration of the ancient prophecies and apocalyptic warnings associated with Denver Airport, we are drawn further into the intricate web of secrets and mysteries that shroud this enigmatic place. The second half of this chapter delves deeper into the symbolism and theories that surround the airport, revealing even more shocking revelations.

One of the most intriguing aspects of Denver Airport is its peculiar layout, which some theorists believe bears a striking resemblance to the sacred geometry found in ancient civilizations. They argue that these deliberate similarities are not mere coincidences, but a deliberate attempt to tap into the ancient wisdom and prophecies of that span of time. Could it be that the builders of the airport, whether knowingly or unknowingly, are trying to harness the power and knowledge of these age-old predictions for their own gain?

The puzzling murals that adorn the walls of the Great Hall continue to captivate our imagination and leave us with questions about their hidden meanings. One mural, titled "Peace and Harmony with Nature," depicts children surrounded by a destroyed industrial complex, with a fallen firefighter at the forefront. The stark contrast between destruction and innocence begs the question: are we being warned about the consequences of our reckless pursuit of progress and power? Or is there a darker, more ominous message lurking beneath the surface?

Our journey through Denver Airport wouldn't be complete without unraveling the mystery behind the infamous "Gargoyle" statue. With its sinister appearance and glowing red eyes, it has become a symbol of intrigue and speculation. Some theorists propose the statue serves as a guardian, protecting hidden knowledge, or even acting as a time-traveling sentinel. As we peel back the layers of this mystery, the line between reality and fiction becomes increasingly blurred, leaving us eager to uncover the truth that lies beneath the surface.

For the general audience seeking entertainment, Denver Airport offers a thrilling escape from reality. The idea of a secret underground world connected by hidden tunnels fuels their imaginations and sparks their curiosity. Lured by stories of secret societies, government cover-ups, and ancient prophecies, they are propelled into a captivating mystery that promises an exhilarating journey.

Even the most academic and research-oriented readers cannot resist the allure of Denver Airport's mysteries. Approaching the topic with a critical eye, they delve into historical records, scrutinize ancient texts, and cross-reference theories to determine the validity behind the prophecies and apocalyptic warnings associated with the airport. Their pursuit of truth intertwines with the excitement of unveiling secrets, making this journey an irresistible quest for those dedicated to pursuing knowledge.

As we near the conclusion of this chapter, the hidden messages within the walls of Denver Airport hold the potential to shape our understanding of the world. Each theory, connection, and enigma bring us closer to deciphering the puzzle that lies before us. Unraveling these mysteries not only satisfies our thirst for knowledge but also leaves us pondering the implications they may hold for the future of humanity.

THE HIDDEN TUNNELS: UNRAVELING THE ENIGMATIC SECRETS OF THE DENVER AIRPORT

As we reach the end of this chapter, the true extent of the prophecies and apocalyptic warnings associated with the Denver Airport remain elusive. The journey, however, is far from over. The next phase of our exploration will lead us deeper into the intricate labyrinth of secrets, as we unravel more shocking revelations that have the power to challenge our perceptions of reality. Stay tuned as we continue down the rabbit hole, guided by the threads of ancient prophecies and enigmatic secrets that will forever alter our understanding of Denver Airport and its significance in the grand tapestry of human history.

Chapter 10: Decoding the Murals

As we delve into the mysterious world of Denver Airport, we come across one of its most controversial and enigmatic features - the murals. Adorning the walls of this peculiar establishment, these artworks have sparked intrigue, speculation, and endless debate among conspiracy theory enthusiasts, skeptics, critical thinkers, and curious minds alike.

To truly understand the meaning behind these murals, it is essential to analyze their symbolism, explore potential hidden messages, and consider the diverse interpretations surrounding them. These artworks have become an integral part of the conspiracy theory culture, igniting the imagination of science fiction and mystery fans, as well as deeply provoking the curiosity of a much wider, general audience seeking entertainment.

One of the most famous murals in Denver Airport is titled "Peace and Harmony with Nature." At first glance, this mural captivates viewers with its vibrant colors and innocent depictions of nature and biodiversity. Yet, closer inspection reveals a more troubling narrative. A conspicuous figure wearing a gas mask, surrounded by a devastated environment, hints at an apocalyptic scenario.

The presence of a dead animal in the foreground and children grieving over extinct species raises questions about the mural's message. Is it a poignant warning about humanity's disregard for the natural world? Or does it represent a hidden agenda, showing a mass extinction event orchestrated by a powerful, malevolent force?

Another mural that has gained notoriety is "Children of the World Dream of Peace." This uplifting artwork depicts children from various cultural backgrounds, dressed in their traditional attire, releasing doves as a symbol of peace. However, as the observer delves deeper, they may notice the looming presence of a militaristic figure wearing a gas mask, holding a menacing sword.

Some theorize that this mural is a visual representation of the New World Order, a secret society aiming to establish global control. The presence of a child sleeping in a coffin-like structure, along with the destruction of historical landmarks in the background, adds fuel to these speculations. Are the children unknowingly taking part in a sinister plan for world domination?

THE HIDDEN TUNNELS: UNRAVELING THE ENIGMATIC SECRETS OF THE DENVER AIRPORT

The symbols within these murals are undeniably thought-provoking, but it is important to approach them with a critical and open mind. While the artist, Leo Tanguma, has offered his own interpretation, it is crucial to consider alternative viewpoints and engage in healthy skepticism. One also acknowledges that art can be subjective, with multiple layers of meaning embedded within it.

Some argue that these murals are merely representations of the artist's creativity and imagination, devoid of any malevolence or hidden messages. They perceive them as a reflection of the human experience, bringing attention to social and environmental issues, and provoking contemplation.

In the second half of this chapter, we will continue our exploration of the hidden meanings of these murals, examining more controversial theories and interesting interpretations. From tales of secret underground bases to connections with ancient civilizations, prepare to have your curiosity piqued and your imagination ignited. Join us as we venture further into the depths of the Denver Airport's mysterious murals, seeking answers and uncovering the truth that lies within.

As we continue our exploration into the hidden meanings of the murals at Denver Airport, we delve deeper into the realm of controversial theories and interesting interpretations. Brace yourselves, for the next mural we encounter is filled with intrigue and mystique.

Titled "In Peace and Harmony with Nature," this mural has stirred up many theories and speculation. The vibrant colors and seemingly innocuous depictions of nature initially catch the eye, drawing us into its imagery. Yet, upon closer examination, a disconcerting narrative emerges. A figure donning a gas mask stands prominently in the frame, surrounded by a devastated environment. The presence of a dead animal in the foreground and grieving children mourning extinct species raises profound questions.

Could this mural be a poignant warning about the consequences of humanity's disregard for the natural world? Is it a reflection of our collective indifference, leading to an imminent apocalypse? Or does it hint at a malevolent force orchestrating a mass extinction event? The ambiguity within these artworks fuels our imagination and compels us to consider the broader implications of their symbolism.

Moving on to another notorious mural entitled "Children of the World Dream of Peace," we encounter an initially uplifting scene. Children from diverse cultural backgrounds, dressed in traditional attire, release doves as symbols of peace. However, beneath the surface of this idyllic tableau lies a more sinister presence. A militaristic figure, donning a gas mask and wielding a menacing sword, ominously looms in the background.

Many conspiracy theorists speculate this mural represents the New World Order—a secret society seeking to establish global control. Including a child sleeping within a coffin-like structure, coupled with the destruction of historical landmarks in the backdrop, further fuels these speculations. Are the innocent children unwitting participants in a grand plan for world domination? This mural, like the others, prompts us to question the deeper significance and hidden agenda behind its seemingly innocent facade.

While these interpretations may seem far-fetched to some, it is crucial to approach them with a critical and open mind. It is within our nature to seek meaning and connect dots, often leading us down unexpected rabbit holes. We must also respect the artist's intentions and acknowledge that art is subjective, open to various layers and interpretations.

For those who view these murals as the product of artistic creativity and imagination, devoid of any malevolence or hidden messages, they see them as catalysts for introspection and social awareness. To them, the paintings lay bare the human experience, shedding light on pressing social and environmental issues.

In the grand tapestry of conspiracy theories and enigmatic art, the murals at Denver Airport have certainly made their mark. They continue to captivate the minds of conspiracy theory enthusiasts, skeptics, and critical thinkers alike. But our journey does not end here. The depths of Denver Airport's mysterious murals still hold many secrets waiting to be uncovered.

In the upcoming chapters, we will explore even more controversial theories, intriguing connections to ancient civilizations, and tales of secret underground bases shrouded in secrecy. Prepare yourselves for a riveting adventure as we dive further into the intricate tapestry of Denver Airport's enigmatic murals. Join us as we seek answers and unveil the truth that lies within these captivating works of art.

THE HIDDEN TUNNELS: UNRAVELING THE ENIGMATIC SECRETS OF THE DENVER AIRPORT

There you have it, dear readers—a mere glimpse into the hidden world of Denver Airport murals. May this journey inspire your curiosity, challenge your beliefs, and ignite your imagination. Intrigue awaits as we embark on our quest to unravel the enigmatic secrets of Denver Airport. Stay tuned for the chapters to come, for the truth beckons.

Chapter 11: The Elusive Masonic Connection

Uncover the alleged ties between Denver Airport and Freemasonry, examining the symbolism and rituals that have sparked speculation around this secretive organization.

Deep beneath the surface of Denver International Airport lies a network of hidden tunnels. Whispers of their existence have spread among conspiracy theory enthusiasts, skeptics, and curious minds around the world. These tunnels, shrouded in mystery, have given birth to many theories and speculations, including a remarkable claim: a connection between the airport and the enigmatic Freemasons.

Freemasonry, often associated with secret societies and ancient rituals, has long fascinated both believers and skeptics. From the conspiracy-filled imaginations of Hollywood to real-life accounts of influential figures involved in the craft, Freemasonry has become a magnet for those seeking to unravel the truth behind its existence and influence. And the alleged connection between Freemasonry and the Denver Airport only adds to the intrigue.

One of the key elements that has fueled speculation is the abundance of Masonic symbols scattered throughout the airport. As travelers make their way through, they are greeted by mysterious murals and peculiar statues that hint at a deeper meaning. The famous blue horse statue, colloquially known as "Blucifer," stands as a haunting symbol guarding the entrance to the airport. Its glowing red eyes have been interpreted by some as a nod to the all-seeing eye, a prominent symbol in Masonry.

Moving deeper into the airport, one cannot help but notice the intricate murals adorning the walls. These controversial murals depict apocalyptic scenes, with symbols tied to conspiracy theories and secret societies. From the Phoenix rising from the ashes to the children of different ethnic backgrounds avoiding violence, each painting sparks curiosity and further speculation. Some believe that these murals contain hidden messages, perhaps guiding members of the Freemasons or shedding light on their alleged involvement with a New World Order.

But what rituals or ceremonies take place in the depths of Denver Airport's hidden tunnels? Several theories suggest that these underground spaces serve as meeting grounds for Masonic lodges or even act as portals to different dimensions. Reports of strange noises and whispers emanating from the subway system beneath the airport have fueled these theories, creating a captivating narrative for science fiction and mystery fans alike.

The airport's unique layout has also piqued interest in its supposed connection to Freemasonry. Its widely recognized design, resembling a swastika from an aerial perspective, has raised eyebrows and prompted questions. Some theorists suggest that this design was intentional and represents the symbol's ancient significance, while others dismiss it as pure coincidence. The alignment of runways and other structures distinctively has led to further speculation surrounding the airport's hidden purpose.

As this exploration into the alleged Masonic ties at Denver Airport unfolds, it is important to approach the subject with a critical mindset. While symbols and peculiarities may intrigue, it is essential to distinguish between fact and fiction, exploring the fine line that separates truth from elaboration. The second half of this chapter will delve deeper into the hidden tunnels and their connection to Freemasonry, shedding light on the secrets that lie beneath the surface of this enigmatic airport.

...

(End of the first half of Chapter 11: The Elusive Masonic Connection) Deep within the bowels of Denver International Airport, the hidden tunnels beckon, inviting explorers to unravel the secrets they hold. The mysterious connection between Freemasonry and these labyrinthine passages has both skeptics and believers captivated, as they yearn for a glimpse into the enigmatic world that lies beneath.

As one journeys further into the depths of the airport, the hidden tunnels reveal themselves to be more than mere corridors. Rumors of secret rituals, clandestine meetings, and even portals to alternate dimensions have left conspiracy theorists and science fiction enthusiasts alike in a state of perpetual wonder.

Whispers of strange noises and hushed conversations float through the air, emanating from the subway system that intertwines with the hidden tunnels. Some claim to have heard echoes of ancient chants and the faint clinking of ceremonial tools, fueling the belief that these underground spaces serve as meeting grounds for Masonic lodges.

The layout of Denver Airport, with its distinct and controversial design, adds another layer of intrigue to the alleged Masonic connection. While some argue that the swastika-like pattern from an aerial perspective is nothing more than an unfortunate coincidence, others delve into its ancient symbolism. Could it be a deliberate nod to the mysteries of Freemasonry, a subtle hint at the airport's hidden purpose?

In the second half of this chapter, we delve even deeper into the heart of the hidden tunnels and explore their profound connection to Freemasonry. It is here that the true secrets of Denver Airport lie, waiting to be unfurled like ancient scrolls.

Within these secret chambers, hidden away from public view, lies a world beyond our wildest imaginations. Illuminated by the flickering glow of torches, Masonic symbols adorn the walls, creating an atmosphere that feels simultaneously ancient and timeless. Knights Templar crosses, the All-Seeing Eye, and intricate geometric patterns intertwine, hinting at an esoteric knowledge attainable only by those started into the craft.

But what purpose do these tunnels serve for the Freemasons? Are they conduits for deep spiritual exploration, leading seekers to profound enlightenment? Or do they serve a more practical purpose, facilitating the clandestine workings of the secret society?

As our exploration continues, testimonies from those who have ventured into the depths of the tunnels emerge. Tales of mysterious encounters and unexplained phenomena surface, further fueling the allure of Denver Airport's hidden chambers. Some speak of ethereal gateways, transporting individuals to other dimensions or even alternate realities, while others recount inexplicable visions, revealing truths that lie beyond our limited human understanding.

Yet, even as we immerse ourselves in this fascinating realm of speculation and mystery, it is crucial to approach the subject with a discerning and critical mindset. Separating truth from fiction becomes a delicate dance, as we navigate the thin line that separates fact from elaborate mythmaking.

For conspiracy theory enthusiasts, skeptics, and critical thinkers alike, the hidden tunnels of Denver Airport offer an opportunity to challenge our preconceived notions and question the boundaries of our knowledge. They invite us to explore the realm of possibility and remind us that pursuing truth is a winding, sometimes treacherous journey.

THE HIDDEN TUNNELS: UNRAVELING THE ENIGMATIC SECRETS OF THE DENVER AIRPORT

As we conclude our exploration of the elusive Masonic connection, we remember that the allure of the unknown lies not only in finding answers but also in embracing the limitless realm of questions. The secrets of Denver Airport's hidden tunnels may forever remain shrouded in mystery, locked away in the minds of those who hold their keys. But it is through our collective curiosity and tireless pursuit of truth that we can hope to unravel the enigmatic secrets that lie within.

Chapter 12: Hidden Technology and Time Travel

Delve into the theories proposing advanced technology and time travel experiments taking place beneath the airport, blurring the lines between science fiction and reality.

The Denver Airport: a sprawling complex shrouded in conspiracy theories, mystery, and speculation. While many visitors land at this bustling transportation hub and continue with their journeys, there are those who believe that there is so much more to discover within the depths of its hidden tunnels. Rumors persist about a clandestine world beneath the airport, where advanced technology and time travel experiments are said to be taking place.

As conspiracy theory enthusiasts, skeptics, and critical thinkers, we find ourselves drawn into the enigmatic secrets of Denver Airport. Are these speculations purely products of overactive imaginations, or is there a grain of truth hidden within the shadows? To explore this realm, we must be open to the possibility that science fiction and reality might intertwine in ways we never thought possible.

According to a theory, Denver Airport has hidden advanced technology in its underground tunnels that goes beyond what the public knows. Some believe that these tunnels are not merely for utility or transportation purposes, but serve as gateways to unexplored realms of scientific advancement. It is speculated that these concealed facilities harbor cutting-edge laboratories, secret research projects, and perhaps even teleportation devices.

But where does time travel come into play? The connection between advanced technology and the manipulation of time offers a tantalizing possibility. Some theorize that time travel experiments are being conducted beneath the airport, with scientists and researchers attempting to unlock the secrets of temporal manipulation. Could it be that our perception of time as linear is nothing more than an illusion?

These speculations, while captivating, inevitably raise skeptical eyebrows. Science fiction and conspiracy theories often collide in a battle between the extraordinary and the plausible. However, it is precisely this clash that invites us to question the boundaries of our understanding. Skepticism is healthy, as it prompts us to demand evidence and scrutinize claims. Yet should we dismiss every theory that stretches the limits of our current knowledge?

Science fiction and mystery fans are no stranger to the concept of hidden worlds, secret experiments, and advanced technology. They revel in the allure of the unknown and eagerly explore realms where fantastical ideas intertwine with scientific principles. Denver Airport, with all its controversial narratives, presents an ideal setting for these curious minds to delve into an alternate reality where the improbable may have become possible.

But it is not just the realm of fanatics and enthusiasts that find themselves captivated by the tales spun around Denver Airport. A general audience seeking entertainment and escape from the mundane is equally intrigued by the allure of hidden technologies and time travel possibilities. After all, who doesn't enjoy a captivating mystery that challenges their perception of reality?

Even academic and research-oriented readers can find value in these theories, for they serve as a reminder that scientific inquiry should never become complacent. The world of academia thrives on questioning established norms, challenging assumptions, and pushing the boundaries of knowledge. By exploring these conspiracy theories from an informed perspective, they contribute to the ongoing dialogue between speculative fiction and scientific exploration.

As we venture further into the hidden tunnels of the Denver Airport, the lines between science fiction and reality blur. With each step, we uncover tantalizing clues that hint at the existence of advanced technology and time travel experiments. But what lies at the end of this labyrinth? To find out, we must continue our journey, peering into the unknown with open minds and relentless curiosity.

And so, we leave you here, suspended in anticipation, as we prepare to unveil the second half of this captivating chapter. The secrets of the hidden tunnels at Denver Airport remain elusive, but, dear readers, we will share the discoveries that await us in the depths of this enigmatic realm. Stay tuned for the next installment, for the truth may be closer than we think, and the consequences may be beyond imagination. The hidden tunnels beneath Denver Airport continue to beckon us, drawing us deeper into their mysterious embrace. As we explore this enigmatic realm, the theories surrounding advanced technology and time travel grow more intriguing, blurring the lines between science fiction and reality.

Imagine, if you will, stepping into one of those concealed facilities within the underground labyrinth of tunnels. The atmosphere is filled with excitement and nervousness as you step into an innovative laboratory. The latest scientific equipment and futuristic gadgets line the walls, their purpose shrouded in secrecy. There are exciting rumors about innovative research that are making you curious and eager to find out more.

One theory suggests that teleportation devices exist within these hidden facilities. These devices, which were once the stuff of science fiction, hold the potential to revolutionize travel as we know it. Imagine being able to transport instantaneously from one location to another, bypassing the time-consuming inconveniences of airports and long-haul flights. It seems like an impossible dream, but within the depths of Denver Airport, it might just be a reality.

But what about time travel? The idea of manipulating time has captured the imaginations of countless scientists, writers, and dreamers throughout the ages. Could the hidden tunnels beneath Denver Airport hold the key to unlocking this extraordinary power? Some believe that time travel experiments are underway, bridging the gap between what we perceive as past, present, and future. It's a notion that challenges the very fabric of our understanding and propels us into a realm of possibility that was once deemed impossible.

As we tread cautiously through the interconnected web of conspiracy and speculation, skepticism is a companion we cannot afford to abandon. It urges us to question, to demand evidence, to examine each theory through the lens of logical reasoning. And yet, it is also skepticism that pushes us to consider the extraordinary, to contemplate the notion that perhaps our current knowledge does not encompass all that exists within the vast universe.

Conspiracy theories and speculative fiction have long held a place in the hearts of enthusiasts and fans alike. These realms of hidden worlds and secret experiments ignite our sense of wonder and allow us to explore the realm of the impossible. The Denver Airport, with its controversial reputation and whispered secrets, serves as the perfect backdrop for our journey into a world where the boundaries of reality and fiction merge.

This intriguing exploration goes beyond entertainment. Even for the most research-oriented minds among us, these theories offer a reminder that scientific inquiry should never stagnate. The pursuit of knowledge demands that we challenge established norms and venture into uncharted territories. By engaging with these ideas, we contribute to the ongoing dialogue between speculative fiction and scientific exploration, pushing the boundaries of what we thought was possible.

And now, dear readers, as we approach the conclusion of this captivating chapter, the enigma of the hidden tunnels takes on a new depth. The answers we seek may be hidden just beyond our reach, but we are determined to uncover the truth that beckons from the depths of this enigmatic realm.

As we prepare to depart from this chapter, let us hold on to our open minds and relentless curiosity. The hidden technology and time travel experiments that lie within Denver Airport remain shrouded in secrecy, but the journey we have embarked upon has brought us one step closer to unraveling these enigmatic secrets. Stay tuned for the next installment, where the truth may be revealed, and the consequences may surpass our wildest imaginations.

Chapter 13: The Cryptic Runways

Explore the peculiarities surrounding the runways at Denver Airport, including their unusual layout and alleged connections to ancient civilizations.

As we delve into the mysterious realm of the Denver International Airport, our focus now turns to an aspect that continues to captivate the imagination of conspiracy theory enthusiasts, skeptics, critical thinkers, and curious minds alike – the enigmatic runways. These massive concrete aprons stretch across the vast plains surrounding the airport, leaving us pondering their peculiar layout and alleged ties to ancient civilizations.

At first glance, the runways appear just as any other runways you might find at an airport – long, wide, and ready to accommodate departing and arriving aircraft. But it doesn't take long for the discerning eye to notice something peculiar about their design. The runways at Denver Airport are shaped like a swastika.

Yes, you read that correctly. Instead of the standard parallel or intersecting runways, the layout at Denver Airport forms a shape that bears eerie resemblance to the controversial symbol that has deep historical roots. Now, before diving into a myriad of wild theories and speculations, it's important to note that the intention behind this design has been vehemently denied by airport officials. According to them, the swastika-like shape is purely coincidental and unintentional.

However, conspiracy theories and speculation are rarely deterred by official explanations. Some theorists argue that the swastika's association with ancient cultures predates its connection to Nazi Germany and suggests that the airport's design could be an intentional homage to these historical origins. They point to the symbol's use in various cultures worldwide, including ancient Hindu, Jain, and Buddhist traditions, where it represents auspiciousness, good fortune, and harmony.

Drawing on this, some speculate that the runways, with their swastika-like design, may serve as a hidden tribute to the past, a symbolic connection to greater mysteries and ancient civilizations. Could this peculiar layout be a deliberate nod to lost knowledge? Or does it simply reflect an architect's creative whim?

To add fuel to the fire, the runways at Denver Airport also boast an intricate system of markings and symbols. A labyrinth of strange patterns, unknown symbols, and even cryptic codes are etched into the runways themselves, further fueling the belief that there is more than meets the eye in this otherwise mundane aspect of an airport.

One theory suggests that these markings serve as hidden messages to those in the know, secret codes that could be deciphered by those who possess the key to unlocking their meaning. Could the runways, with their mysterious symbols, be signaling important information concealed by the powers that be? Are they part of an elaborate puzzle waiting to be unraveled?

As we explore the cryptic runways at Denver Airport, it becomes clear that they hold captivating secrets and raise more questions than answers. Are they a mere coincidence, a testimony to the power of pareidolia, where our minds seek patterns even where there are none? Or could they be meaningful symbols, deliberately integrated into the fabric of the airport, hinting at a hidden world of ancient knowledge and intricate conspiracies?

In the second half of this chapter, we will delve deeper into the alleged connections between Denver Airport's runways and ancient civilizations. Prepare to unravel the enigmatic secrets that lie beneath the surface, as we uncover the hidden history and explore the mysteries that lie within these concrete enigmas.

As we continue our exploration of the mysterious runways at Denver Airport, we peer ever deeper into the connections between these concrete enigmas and ancient civilizations. The allure of hidden history and cryptic secrets lingers in the air, fueling our curiosity to uncover the truth that lies beneath the surface.

The alleged ties between the runways and ancient civilizations have captivated the imaginations of conspiracy theorists, skeptics, and critical thinkers alike. Some believe that the unique markings and symbols etched into the runways hold hidden messages, waiting to be deciphered by those with the knowledge and the key. These cryptic codes, some argue, could be the breadcrumbs leading to deeper truths and greater mysteries.

Intriguingly, several researchers have drawn connections between the runways and the ancient Nazca Lines in Peru. Just as the Nazca Lines, created by the Nazca people over a thousand years ago, depict various animals and shapes visible only from an aerial perspective, the runways at Denver Airport seem to possess a similar hidden language. Could these enigmatic symbols be part of a long-lost tradition, a method of communication used by ancient civilizations to convey messages beyond the comprehension of the average observer?

Some conspiracy theorists have gone further, proposing that the runways serve as a secret landing site for extraterrestrial beings or even time travelers. They speculate that the assortment of markings and symbols on these vast concrete canvases might be a means of navigation for otherworldly entities or a code for unlocking the mysteries of time and space. While these ideas may seem far-fetched to many, they undeniably add an intriguing layer of science fiction to the already mysterious narrative.

However, it is crucial to approach these theories with a critical mindset, acknowledging that concrete evidence is scarce. The temptation of the unknown is hard to resist, especially in fields where speculation holds sway. Skeptics argue that the peculiar layout and markings on the runways are simply a product of pareidolia, the phenomenon where our minds perceive patterns and symbols even where none truly exist.

The undeniable fact remains that the runways at Denver Airport continue to inspire fascination and intrigue. Regardless of one's stance on conspiracy theories, the symbolic resonance of ancient knowledge, or the existence of extraterrestrial life, the powerful impact that these cryptic runways have on our collective imagination.

In conclusion, the mysteries surrounding the runways at Denver Airport are far from solved. The alleged connections to ancient civilizations, the enigmatic symbols etched into their surfaces, and the lingering questions about their true purpose continue to provoke wonder and curiosity. Whether they are a mere coincidence or intentional nods to a hidden world beyond our comprehension, one thing is certain – the runways at Denver Airport will always hold a place in the realm of intrigue and fascination. So, let us embark on this journey of unraveling the enigmatic secrets that lie within as we peel back the layers of history and untangle the intricate web of mysteries surrounding these concrete enigmas.

But remember, dear reader, the truth may be elusive and frustratingly opaque. Only by maintaining an open mind, grounded skepticism, and a thirst for knowledge can we hope to uncover even a fraction of the profound secrets that lie beneath the surface of Denver Airport's cryptic runways.

Chapter 14: The DIA Conspiracy Timeline

From its inception, the Denver International Airport (DIA) has been a subject of fascination and speculation. Over the years, a multitude of conspiracy theories have emerged, swirling around the airport like a whirlwind of enigmatic secrets. In this chapter, we dive into the timeline of events and controversies associated with DIA, uncovering key moments that have fueled these conspiracy theories.

1995 marked the grand opening of DIA, which was an extravagant affair. Draped in mystery, the airport's dedication ceremony featured peculiar symbols and artworks that immediately intrigued conspiracy theorists. The most widely debated piece was the iconic "Mustang" statue, with its glowing red eyes, known to some as the "Bluecifer" or "Lucifer" statue. The presence of this seemingly ominous artwork set the stage for the curious events that followed.

In 2007, DIA became a hotbed of conspiracy theory discussions when a strange underground complex was uncovered. Officially termed as an automated baggage handling system, this subterranean labyrinth of tunnels raised eyebrows and suspicions. Theories quickly emerged, suggesting that these tunnels were part of a nefarious plan, possibly used for secret government operations or even as a hideout for the fabled Illuminati.

The controversy surrounding DIA reached new heights in 2011 when the airport unveiled its new terminal renovation project. The blueprints included cryptic markings and symbols that sparked a surge of conspiracy theories. Some speculated that these symbols were coded messages, pointing to a hidden agenda or an apocalyptic event. Others believed they were evidence of an alien presence or a clue to the existence of a secret society.

Moving forward to 2012, a series of mysterious murals took center stage at DIA, further fueling the conspiracy fire. Painted by artist Leo Tanguma, these vivid and thought-provoking artworks showcased themes of war, death, and global catastrophe. Advocates of conspiracy theories argued these murals hinted at a hidden message, suggesting that the powers-that-be were preparing for a cataclysmic event or a new world order.

In 2016, DIA faced another controversial turn of events when a time capsule, buried during the airport's dedication ceremony, was scheduled to be opened. Conspiracy theorists eagerly awaited this moment, convinced that it would unveil long-held secrets. However, at the last minute, the airport officials postponed the opening indefinitely, leading to a flurry of speculation about the contents and their potentially earth-shattering significance.

As the years rolled on, DIA continued to be fertile ground for conspiracy theories. In 2018, rumors emerged about secret bunkers and tunnels beneath the airport, supposedly housing a shadow government or clandestine organizations. Claims of unusual airport noises, unidentified flying objects, and covert military operations only added to the intrigue and intensity of the theories surrounding DIA.

And so, we find ourselves suspended in a web of unanswered questions, wrapped in the unknown's allure. The tangled web of conspiracy theories surrounding DIA is an enigma that continues to captivate the minds of conspiracy theory enthusiasts, skeptics, and critical thinkers alike. As we venture into the second half of this chapter, we delve deeper into the layers of mystery and explore the various conspiracy narratives that define Denver International Airport.

(Note: The second half of this chapter will be added in the next installment.) The persistent allure of the Denver International Airport (DIA) conspiracy theories is a testament to the power of the unknown. It is within this realm of mystery that we continue our exploration, delving deeper into the layers of intrigue that have enveloped this enigmatic airport.

Among the many theories surrounding DIA, one that has captivated the minds of conspiracy theorists is the alleged existence of a vast underground bunker network, supposedly hidden beneath the airport. According to this narrative, these underground tunnels serve as a secret base for a shadow government or clandestine organizations. Whispers of military installations, government experiments, and covert operations have infiltrated the conversations surrounding DIA, further fueling the speculation.

Much like the underground complex unveiled in 2007, these rumored tunnels have become a focal point for conspiracy theorists seeking evidence of a hidden agenda. It is through these tunnels that theories of mind control experiments, alien encounters, and even time travel have emerged, intertwining reality and fiction with a fascinating allure.

Adding to the intrigue, reports of unusual noises emanating from the airport have only heightened curiosity and speculation. Witnesses claim to have heard unexplained rumblings and eerie sounds echoing through the halls of DIA. Some conspiracy theorists have even suggested a connection between these noises and the alleged secret tunnels, positing that they result from secret experiments or extraterrestrial activity hidden beneath the surface.

But it is not only the underground that has fueled the conspiracy theories surrounding DIA; the skies above the airport have also become a source of fascination. Countless reports of unidentified flying objects (UFOs) hovering near or even directly above the airport have drawn the attention of both skeptics and believers alike. These sightings, paired with bizarre photographs and videos circulating on the internet, have sparked debates about the possibility of extraterrestrial visitations or covert military operations occurring at DIA.

Yet, throughout the years, Denver International Airport has remained tight-lipped about the mounting conspiracy theories, dismissing them as unfounded or mere figments of imagination. Official explanations regarding the underground tunnels revolve around mundane purposes such as baggage handling or transportation systems. The strange symbols and cryptic markings discovered within the blueprints are often attributed to artistic interpretation or architectural design choices.

The constant speculation remains despite these official explanations. Conspiracy theory enthusiasts, skeptics, and critical thinkers alike are all captivated by the tenacious grip of the allure of the unknown. The whispers of hidden agendas, secret societies, and malevolent forces continue to weave their intricate web, encircling Denver International Airport with an air of mystery that refuses to dissipate.

As we reach the conclusion of this chapter, we stand at the precipice of the unknown. The Denver International Airport, with its complex tapestry of controversies, enigmatic symbols, and whispered secrets, has become a treasure trove for those hungry for the mysteries of the world.

Whether these conspiracy theories are born out of a genuine desire to uncover the truth or are merely the result of overactive imaginations, we cannot deny the pull they exert on our collective curiosity. The stories that revolve around DIA, whether grounded or fueled by fiction, add color and intrigue to our lives, reminding us that there is still much we do not know about the world we inhabit.

As we say our goodbyes to Denver International Airport, let us not forget that the quest for knowledge, even when it seems impossible or tempting, is an endlessly fascinating journey. The next conspiracy theory may be just around the corner, waiting to unravel the enigmatic secrets that lie hidden in plain sight.

Chapter 15: Bunkers and Survivalism

Deep below the bustling Denver International Airport lies a vast network of mysterious tunnels, shrouded in rumors and speculation. Conspiracy theorists from around the world have been captivated by the idea of massive underground bunkers lurking beneath the surface, ready to harbor the elite during times of a global crisis. In this chapter, we will delve into the claims surrounding these enigmatic tunnels and explore the ideas of survivalism and hidden agendas tied to them.

The notion of underground bunkers is not new, and throughout history, nations have constructed secret hideouts away from prying eyes. However, the scale of the alleged underground complex beneath Denver Airport is said to dwarf all others. Some theorists claim these bunkers can house the world's political leaders, keeping them safe during cataclysmic events. But are these claims grounded, or are they simply the product of overactive imaginations?

Survivalism, as a way of life, has gained popularity in recent years. With global uncertainties such as climate change, economic instability, and political unrest, it is not surprising that people are seeking ways to protect themselves and their loved ones. The idea of having an underground bunker equipped with essential supplies and resources may seem like a practical solution when faced with potential disasters. But does this concept hold any truth for Denver Airport?

Proponents of the bunker theory point to various pieces of evidence to validate their claims. They argue that the many construction projects and ongoing renovations at the airport are merely a facade. According to them, these activities provide cover for the actual work being done deep underground. Reports of unusual noises, unexplained vibrations, and restricted access in certain areas have only fueled the speculation surrounding this hidden network.

But skeptics raise pertinent questions about the plausibility of such an extensive underground complex. The logistical challenges of constructing such a massive structure without detection seem insurmountable. The airport's proximity to an urban area with a dense population raises concerns about the feasibility of keeping the bunker secret. Shouldn't there be more solid evidence supporting the existence of these underground installations?

Another intriguing aspect of the Denver Airport conspiracy theories is the notion of hidden agendas. Some theorists suggest that these alleged bunkers might not be designed solely for survival. Rather, they propose that there may be clandestine activities taking place within these tunnels, possibly connected to shadowy government operations or even extraterrestrial encounters. Could there be a deeper, more sinister purpose to these hidden tunnels?

As we embark on our exploration of the claims surrounding Denver Airport's mysterious underground bunkers, it is essential to approach this topic with both curiosity and critical thinking. By examining the evidence and considering different perspectives, we can attempt to uncover the truth lurking beneath the surface. In the second half of this chapter, we will delve deeper into the mysteries of these hidden tunnels, revealing startling revelations that challenge our understanding of the world as we know it.

But for now, dear reader, we must pause our investigation. The secrets of Denver Airport's underground complex remain tantalizingly out of reach, beckoning us to unveil the truths that lie hidden in the darkness. Join us in the next part of this chapter as we unravel the enigmatic secrets of Denver Airport. The journey continues, and the surprises that await us will leave you questioning everything you thought you knew. Stay tuned, for there is much more to discover in the depths of the underground...But for now, dear reader, we must pause our investigation. The secrets of Denver Airport's underground complex remain tantalizingly out of reach, beckoning us to unveil the truths that lie hidden in the darkness. Join us in the next part of this chapter as we unravel the enigmatic secrets of Denver Airport. The journey continues, and the surprises that await us will leave you questioning everything you thought you knew. Stay tuned, for there is much more to discover in the depths of the underground.

As we delve deeper into the mysteries of Denver Airport's hidden tunnels, we must confront the various theories surrounding their purpose and existence. One prevailing notion that captures the imagination is that these underground bunkers serve as a refuge for the global elite during times of a global crisis. This notion, however, raises important questions.

If there truly are massive underground bunkers beneath the airport, we must ask ourselves: who gets to seek shelter in these hidden chambers? Are they reserved solely for the world's political leaders and influential figures, leaving the general population vulnerable? The implications of such an arrangement are chilling, as it suggests a stark divide between the privileged few and the masses left to face the perils of an uncertain world.

The feasibility of constructing and maintaining such a massive complex without drawing attention seems dubious. Denver Airport is a bustling hub, with constant activity and thousands of people passing through every day. The scale of secrecy required to sustain this alleged underground network in the face of regular airport operations and public scrutiny is mind-boggling. It challenges not only the logistical challenges but also the moral implications of hiding such a resource from those in need.

Skeptics contend that the absence of substantial evidence backing the existence of these underground installations creates uncertainty about their reality. Conspiracies often rely on circumstantial evidence, anecdotal accounts, and ambiguous claims that leave room for interpretation. In a world where information is readily available at our fingertips, the lack of concrete proof fuels skepticism among many.

However, the absence of clear evidence should not dismiss the curiosity surrounding Denver Airport's hidden tunnels. We consider that in a world full of secrets and hidden agendas, the truth often eludes us, buried beneath layers of misinformation and concealment. It is this veil of uncertainty that makes the rumors and speculation surrounding the airport's underground complex captivating.

One aspect of the conspiracy theories that adds another layer of intrigue is the notion of hidden agendas. Some theorists propose that the purpose of these alleged bunkers goes beyond mere survivalism. They believe that clandestine activities may be taking place deep within these tunnels, possibly tied to shadowy government operations or even encounters with extraterrestrial beings.

While these ideas may seem far-fetched to some, they cannot be easily dismissed. History has shown that governments engage in covert operations and secret experiments, often shielded from public knowledge. The blurred line between fact and fiction may be where the truth lies hidden, waiting for intrepid investigators to uncover its secrets.

As we conclude our exploration of the claims surrounding Denver Airport's mysterious underground bunkers, we are left with a multitude of questions. The existence and purpose of these hidden tunnels remain shrouded in uncertainty, challenging us to think critically, question conventional narratives, and seek the truth beyond the surface.

Join us in future chapters as we continue our journey through the shadows, unraveling enigmatic secrets and unraveling the mysteries that lie beneath the surface. The hidden tunnels of Denver Airport are just the beginning, and the world is full of hidden wonders waiting to be revealed. Open your mind and prepare yourself for the unknown, for the truth may be stranger than fiction. Let us embark on this quest together, for the journey into the depths of mystery has only just begun.

Chapter 16: Disproving the Theories

Denver International Airport is no stranger to controversy. It has become a breeding ground for conspiracy theories, sparking the imaginations of conspiracy enthusiasts and skeptics alike. From its unusual art installations to its hidden tunnels and secret underground bunkers, the facility has captured the attention of curious minds and those who enjoy a good mystery.

In this chapter, we aim to take a critical look at the claims and evidence put forward by conspiracy theorists, offering alternative explanations and debunking some of the most pervasive myths. We'll explore the fascinating world of conspiracy theories surrounding Denver Airport and challenge the assumptions behind them.

One prevalent theory revolves around a supposed secret underground tunnel system beneath the airport. Proponents of this theory claim that the tunnels are used for clandestine purposes, ranging from government operations to extraterrestrial encounters. While the idea of hidden tunnels is undoubtedly intriguing, many experts have studied the blueprint of the airport and found no evidence to support such claims. Engineers and architects have concluded that the tunnels primarily serve practical purposes, such as housing utility systems and luggage transportation.

Another widely held belief is that the artwork displayed throughout the airport contains hidden messages and symbols connected to secret societies or even the Illuminati. Admittedly, some of the artwork is peculiar and open to interpretation, but this does not indicate a hidden agenda. Artists often strive to provoke thought and generate discussion through their creations. The art at Denver Airport can be seen as an attempt to elicit a sense of wonder and curiosity, rather than a sinister plot of global influence.

One of the most pervasive myths surrounding Denver Airport is the notion that it is a hub for secret government activities. Conspiracy theories suggest that the facility houses top-secret projects or acts as a refuge for elite individuals during catastrophic events. However, the reality is far less dramatic. As a bustling airport and transportation hub, it is subject to strict regulations and oversight from multiple agencies. It is unlikely that covert government activities could be concealed on such a scale.

THE HIDDEN TUNNELS: UNRAVELING THE ENIGMATIC SECRETS OF THE DENVER AIRPORT

The infamous blue Mustang statue that greets visitors at the airport has also been the subject of speculation. Many claim that it symbolizes the Four Horsemen of the Apocalypse or represents death and destruction. While the statue is undeniably imposing, its intended meaning is far less sinister. The artist, Luis Jiménez, aimed to depict the spirit of the American West with his creation. It may evoke mixed emotions, but there is little evidence to support the apocalyptic interpretations.

As we delve deeper into the world of conspiracy theories surrounding Denver Airport, it becomes apparent that a healthy dose of skepticism is essential. While it is undoubtedly entertaining to entertain these enigmatic notions, it is crucial to approach them with critical thinking and a willingness to dig beyond surface-level explanations. The allure of mystery and the unknown is a powerful force, but we must not let it overshadow reason and evidence-based analysis.

In the second half of this chapter, we will continue to explore alternative explanations and further debunk the theories surrounding Denver Airport. Brace yourselves as we peel back the layers of deception and unveil the truth behind these captivating enigmas. But for now, let us pause and reflect on the intricate web of conspiracy theories that have captivated our minds and stirred our imaginations. The journey is not over yet; it is merely the beginning of a deeper understanding. In the second half of this chapter, let us dive even deeper into the mysterious world of the Denver Airport and continue our exploration of alternative explanations and further debunk the theories that have captivated our minds.

One theory that has gained considerable attention is the claim that the airport's runways are designed in the shape of a swastika. While it may seem unsettling at first glance, this theory is easily debunked with a simple understanding of airport operations. The runways are oriented based on prevailing winds, geographical limitations, and the airport's capacity to handle multiple aircraft. The layout of runways is a complex process that involves the collaboration of engineers, aviation experts, and air traffic controllers, not some hidden message embedded within the airport's design.

Another intriguing theory centers on the murals that adorn the walls of Denver Airport. Some suggest that these artworks depict a hidden story of a New World Order or impending doom. However, a closer analysis reveals a different narrative altogether. These murals, created by artists Leo Tanguma and Gary Sweeney, use powerful imagery to explore themes of peace, diversity, and environmental stewardship. They spark conversations about human rights, global unity, and the preservation of our planet. While open to interpretation, these murals are not evidence of a secret society trying to control the world.

Among the laundry list of conspiracy theories surrounding the Denver Airport, another popular belief is that its design mimics the shape of a swastika when viewed from above. However, this claim is based on a distorted perception of the airport's layout. The airport's terminals and concourses are designed in multiple linear formations, resulting in a somewhat unique shape when viewed from an aerial perspective. Any resemblance to a swastika is purely coincidental and not indicative of any hidden agenda.

There is one theory that stands out in its audacity and scale—the idea that Denver Airport houses an underground city. According to this theory, a labyrinth of tunnels and chambers is supposed to exist beneath the airport, housing everything from government bunkers to alien bases. However, extensive investigations and studies conducted by experts have found no evidence to support these claims. The airport's underground spaces primarily serve as utility corridors for heating, ventilation, and electrical systems. These corridors are essential for the smooth operations of the airport and are not part of a vast clandestine network.

As we wrap up our exploration of the conspiracy theories surrounding Denver Airport, it is vital to acknowledge the undeniable allure of mystery and the supernatural. These ideas fuel our imagination and give rise to captivating narratives. However, we must always remember to approach such theories with skepticism and a critical mindset. It is tempting to believe in grand tales of hidden societies, secret tunnels, and extraterrestrial encounters, but evidence and reason must prevail over fantastical notions.

In conclusion, Denver Airport, while enigmatic and intriguing, is not a hub for hidden agendas or sinister plots. It is a vibrant transportation hub, subject to regulations and oversight like any significant public infrastructure. The conspiracy theories that surround it are a testament to the power of human imagination and our innate desire for answers. So, let us be curious, let us ponder, but above all, let us seek truth grounded in evidence and critical thinking.

THE HIDDEN TUNNELS: UNRAVELING THE ENIGMATIC SECRETS OF THE DENVER AIRPORT

As we conclude this chapter, we urge you, the curious reader, to continue questioning, exploring, and unraveling the enigmatic secrets that capture our collective imagination. The journey doesn't end here; it is only the beginning of a world filled with endless possibilities and fascinating mysteries waiting to be unraveled. Embrace your critical thinking, challenge the assumptions, and keep seeking the truth, for it is in pursuing

knowledge that we uncover the most extraordinary revelations.

Chapter 17: Inside the Mind of a Conspiracy Theorist

Have you ever found yourself captivated by a conspiracy theory, eagerly delving into the enigmatic world of hidden agendas and secret societies? If so, you're certainly not alone. Throughout history, countless individuals have been drawn to the allure of uncovering the truth behind elaborate conspiracies, and Denver Airport is no exception. In this chapter, we will explore the psychology behind conspiracy theories, peering into the depths of the human mind to understand what drives individuals to believe in these mysterious narratives.

At first glance, conspiracy theories might seem irrational or even absurd to some. Why would anyone willingly embrace ideas that defy conventional logic? The answer lies in the intricate web of motives and biases that shape our perspectives. Conspiracy theories, motives often revolve around the human desire for certainty, control, and a sense of belonging.

Uncertainty can unsettle, prompting the need for explanations that provide a semblance of order in an unpredictable world. Conspiracy theories offer a convenient explanation, creating a framework where events can be neatly connected, and chaotic occurrences can be attributed to deliberate actions. By assigning a hidden hand behind every major event or societal change, conspiracy theories provide a comforting sense of certainty in an otherwise perplexing reality.

Control is another fundamental human motivation that influences our susceptibility to conspiracy theories. In a world filled with complexities and power imbalances, the notion of an all-powerful puppet master orchestrating events can be strangely empowering. It gives individuals a sense of agency, allowing them to believe that they possess insider knowledge that others do not. By associating themselves with a secret society or revealing the supposed truths withheld by mainstream sources, conspiracy theorists can regain a sense of control and influence over their own lives.

The need for belonging profoundly affects our propensity for conspiracy theories. Human beings are social creatures, constantly seeking connections and a shared sense of identity with others. Conspiracy theories provide a unique opportunity for like-minded individuals to form communities, giving them a sense of camaraderie and purpose. These communities offer a space where individuals can reinforce their beliefs, share evidence, and support each other in the face of skepticism or criticism from the outside world.

However, it would be a mistake to assume that everyone who believes in conspiracy theories is driven solely by motives or biases. Cognitive processes also play a crucial role in shaping our beliefs. Confirmation bias, for instance, leads individuals to seek and accept information that aligns with their pre-existing beliefs, while rejecting or dismissing contradictory evidence. This cognitive tendency reinforces and strengthens conspiracy theories, making it challenging to break the cycle of belief even in the face of counterarguments.

The allure of uncovering hidden truths, the desire for certainty and control, the need for belonging, and the influence of cognitive biases—these elements intertwine within the psychology of conspiracy theories. As we continue exploring the enigmatic secrets of Denver Airport, we will dive deeper into the minds of conspiracy theorists, shedding light on the fascinating intricacies that drive their unwavering beliefs. Get ready to embark on a journey where the lines between fact and fiction blur, and the hidden tunnels within human perception are laid bare.

As we delve further into the enigmatic secrets of conspiracy theories, we uncover the intricate layers of the human mind that contribute to their allure. From the desire for certainty and control to the need for belonging and the influence of cognitive biases, the psychology behind conspiracy theories is a fascinating tapestry that continues to captivate curious minds.

One of the driving forces behind the unwavering beliefs of conspiracy theorists is the allure of uncovering hidden truths. The idea of peering behind the curtain and revealing the secrets that others are unaware of can be exhilarating. It taps into our innate curiosity, our thirst for knowledge, and our fascination with the unknown. Whether it's uncovering the alleged hidden tunnels beneath Denver Airport or unraveling the mystery behind the moon landing, conspiracy theories provide a sense of adventure and discovery that can be incredibly enticing.

But what is it about conspiracy theories that can make them so captivating, even to skeptics and critical thinkers? Part of it lies in the inherent desire for certainty. In a world that can often feel chaotic and unpredictable, the need for explanations that provide order and structure becomes paramount. Conspiracy theories offer a convenient narrative that connects disparate events, attributing them to the actions of a hidden hand. This creates a semblance of certainty, even in the face of confusion or complexity.

Control also plays a significant role in the appeal of conspiracy theories. In a society characterized by power imbalances, the notion of a puppet master with ultimate power can be strangely empowering. By associating oneself with the supposed truth or secret society, individuals regain a sense of agency and influence over their own lives. It gives them a feeling of being privy to insider knowledge, elevating their status above those who remain ignorant.

But perhaps one of the most interesting factors that draws individuals to conspiracy theories is the need for belonging. Human beings are social creatures, continuously seeking connections and a shared sense of identity. Conspiracy theories provide a unique opportunity for like-minded individuals to form communities, creating a sense of camaraderie and purpose. These communities serve as safe spaces where beliefs can be reinforced, evidence can be shared, and support can be found in the face of external skepticism or criticism.

As we navigate through the depths of the human mind, cognitive biases also play a crucial role in shaping our beliefs. Confirmation bias, for instance, leads us to seek and accept information that aligns with our pre-existing beliefs while dismissing contradictory evidence. This cognitive tendency not only reinforces and strengthens conspiracy theories but also makes it challenging to break the cycle of belief.

In conclusion, the allure of conspiracy theories lies in the intricate web of human motives, biases, and cognitive processes that shape our perspectives. The desire for certainty, control, and a sense of belonging, coupled with the influence of confirmation bias, intertwine to create a captivating narrative. Whether you are a conspiracy theory enthusiast, skeptic, critical thinker, or simply curious about the mysteries of our world, exploring the psychology behind these enigmatic narratives invites us to question and examine the hidden tunnels within our own perception.

As we bring this chapter to a close, we leave you understanding that the complexity of conspiracy theories extends beyond their surface-level allure. By delving into the depths of the human mind, we can unravel the enigmatic secrets of why individuals so fervently believe in hidden agendas. But the journey does not end here. There is still much to uncover, and Denver Airport is just the beginning. So, stay curious, keep questioning, and remain open to the intriguing intersections of fact and fiction that lie ahead.

Chapter 18: The Economic Impact of the DIA Conspiracy

With conspiracy theories, few places have captured the imagination quite like the Denver International Airport (DIA). Nestled amidst the vast plains of Colorado, this architectural marvel has captivated conspiracy theorists and skeptics alike with its enigmatic reputation. And while the truth behind the conspiracy theories remains elusive, there's no denying the economic impact they have had on the airport and the surrounding region.

For conspiracy theory enthusiasts, the allure of DIA lies in the hidden tunnels and underground facilities that supposedly house everything from secret government operations to alien interactions. These theories have attracted a dedicated following, drawing visitors from far and wide who are eager to uncover the mysteries hidden beneath the surface. The intrigue surrounding the airport has become a tourism boom, with visitors flocking to take part in guided tours, lectures, and even conspiracy-themed events.

This surge in tourism has undoubtedly benefited the local economy. Hotels, restaurants, and businesses in the Denver area have seen a significant increase in revenue as curious minds and conspiracy enthusiasts pour in. Tour operators now offer specialized tours that explore the hidden tunnels and highlight conspiracy theories, catering to the demand for an unforgettable experience. The airport itself has embraced its mysterious reputation, capitalizing on the intrigue through merchandise sales and incorporating subtle nods to the conspiracy theories throughout the terminal.

However, the economic impact of the DIA conspiracy is not purely positive. Skeptics and critical thinkers argue that the focus on these theories distracts from the true economic potential of the airport and the region. Instead of channeling resources into tourism based on conspiracy theories, they believe efforts should be directed towards promoting the airport as a gateway to the Rockies, fostering collaboration between businesses, and attracting industries that can contribute to the local economy in a more sustainable manner.

The enigmatic reputation of Denver Airport has also caught the attention of science fiction and mystery fans. Books, movies, and even video games have been inspired by conspiracy theories, further fueling interest in the airport. The influence extends beyond entertainment, as academic and research-oriented readers delve into the intricate web of theories, examining them through a critical lens. This academic intrigue has encouraged scholarly debates and studies surrounding the societal impact of conspiracy theories.

While the DIA conspiracy theories have undoubtedly affected the airport and the region's economy, it is essential to evaluate both the pros and cons of this enigmatic reputation. This chapter seeks to explore the economic influence and tourism boost driven by conspiracy theories, highlighting the benefits for local businesses and the excitement it brings to curious minds. Yet, it is equally important to consider skeptics' concerns, and the potential lost opportunities in favor of a more sustainable economic approach.

As we delve deeper into the economic impact of the DIA conspiracy, it is crucial to assess the multiple perspectives surrounding this enigmatic reputation. With tourist dollars flowing into the region and conspiracy enthusiasts uncovering hidden truths, it remains to be seen whether the economic influence of the DIA conspiracy will continue to prosper or if a different approach is necessary for sustained growth. In the following section, we will dissect the pros and cons of this captivating phenomenon and its true impact on Denver Airport and its surrounding communities.

The economic impact of the Denver International Airport (DIA) conspiracy theories is a multifaceted phenomenon that continues to intrigue and divide individuals from various backgrounds and perspectives. While the surge in tourism and revenue has undoubtedly benefited local businesses and the airport itself, there are valid concerns regarding the diversion of resources and missed opportunities for sustainable economic growth.

On one hand, conspiracy theory enthusiasts and curious minds have flocked to DIA, drawn by the allure of hidden tunnels and secret government operations. These individuals have played a crucial role in bolstering the local economy, with hotels, restaurants, and businesses in the Denver area experiencing a significant increase in revenue. The demand for guided tours and conspiracy-themed events has caused the rise of specialized tour operators, who cater to the curiosity and thirst for discovery exhibited by visitors. The airport has cleverly embraced its enigmatic reputation, capitalizing on the intrigue through merchandise sales and subtle nods to the conspiracy theories within the terminal. These endeavors not only contribute to the economic prosperity of the region but also provide an unforgettable experience for those who are captivated by the mysteries hidden beneath the surface of DIA.

However, skeptics and critical thinkers argue that the focus on conspiracy theories detracts from the true economic potential of the airport and the region. Instead of directing resources towards tourism based on these theories, they believe efforts should be redirected towards promoting DIA as a gateway to the Rockies, fostering collaboration between businesses, and attracting industries that can contribute to the local economy in a more sustainable manner. Skeptics raise valid concerns about diverting resources away from other potentially lucrative ventures, as well as the potential impact on the airport's long-term growth and viability.

The economic impact of the DIA conspiracy extends beyond the local economy. Science fiction and mystery fans have been captivated by the enigmatic reputation of the airport, leading to the inspiration of books, movies, and even video games. The influence of these conspiracy theories has transcended entertainment, sparking academic interest and research on the societal impact of conspiracy theories. Scholars and researchers engage in debates and studies surrounding these theories, examining them through a critical lens. This academic intrigue fosters intellectual exploration and encourages deeper analysis of the broader implications of conspiracy theories, beyond their economic influence.

As we assess the entire economic impact, while the DIA conspiracy theories have brought substantial benefits to the airport and the surrounding communities, there are valid concerns that merit consideration. Balancing the allure of tourism and revenue with a sustainable economic approach is of utmost importance for the long-term growth and prosperity of the region, not only economically but also to foster a vibrant and diverse community.

In conclusion, the economic impact of the DIA conspiracy theories cannot be ignored or dismissed lightly. The surge in tourism and revenue has undeniably benefited local businesses, providing an economic boost. However, skeptics raise important concerns about the diversion of resources and missed opportunities for sustainable economic growth. The allure of the conspiracy theories has sparked intellectual curiosity and academic inquiry, extending well beyond entertainment. As we navigate the second half of this chapter, it is crucial to consider the multiple perspectives surrounding this enigmatic reputation, evaluating both the pros and cons it brings to the Denver Airport and its surrounding communities. By doing so, we can gain a comprehensive understanding of the economic influence and tourism boost generated by the DIA conspiracy theories, while also reflecting upon the potential need for a more balanced and sustainable approach for the future.

Chapter 19: The Future of Denver Airport

As we delve into the enigmatic secrets of Denver Airport, it's impossible not to ponder what lies ahead for this intriguing location. With its tumultuous reputation, the potential developments and changes that could occur at Denver Airport are both captivating and mysterious.

Speculation runs rampant within the world of conspiracy theorists, skeptics, and critical thinkers, each with their own unique take on what the future may hold. Some believe that the airport will continue to be shrouded in mystery, forever concealing hidden tunnels and secret societies. Others argue that advancements in technology and increased transparency will debunk the rumors and bring about a new era of understanding.

For those curious minds who have followed the Denver Airport saga, it's no secret that science fiction and mystery fans are drawn to the allure of this place. The airport itself, with its elaborate murals depicting apocalyptic scenes, has become a setting ripe for imaginative storytelling. Countless works of fiction have been inspired by the airport's mysteries, fueling the fascination of readers seeking entertainment within the realms of the unknown.

But what about the general audience, those who may not be well-versed in the conspiracies surrounding Denver Airport? As time goes on, this peculiar place might transcend its reputation and become something more. Imagine a future where the airport becomes a virtual museum, inviting visitors to explore its secrets through interactive exhibits and immersive experiences. The line between reality and fiction could blur, captivating not only conspiracy theorists but also the wider public.

The academic and research-oriented readers cannot be overlooked in this discussion. The controversies surrounding Denver Airport have led to scholarly investigations and inquiries about the airport's purpose and origins. With new technologies and research methods, answers to the questions that have perplexed minds for decades might finally be within reach. This eager audience awaits new discoveries and theories that could shed light on the truth hidden beneath the surface.

So, what lies beyond the present for Denver Airport? The future trajectory of this enigmatic location is both uncertain and tantalizing. As new generations of critical thinkers and curious minds emerge, they will undoubtedly bring fresh perspective and insight into the mysteries that surround us.

In the second half of this chapter, we will further explore the theories, developments, and potential scenarios that might unfold at Denver Airport. The surprises and revelations that lie ahead are sure to astound and captivate even the most skeptical minds. Until then, let us immerse ourselves in the speculation surrounding the enigmatic secrets of this remarkable place, for its allure knows no bounds.

As we delve deeper into the enigmatic secrets of Denver Airport, a world of possibilities emerges. The future trajectory of this remarkable place is both uncertain and tantalizing, leaving conspiracy theorists, skeptics, and critical thinkers on the edge of their seats. In the first half of this chapter, we explored the captivating allure that the airport holds for science fiction and mystery fans, as well as the potential for a virtual museum experience that blurs the line between reality and fiction.

But what about the general audience, those who may not be well-versed in the conspiracies surrounding Denver Airport? As time goes on, this peculiar place might transcend its reputation and become something more. Picture a future where the airport becomes more than just a transportation hub, but a destination. Imagine curated walking tours that highlight the airport's history and secrets, providing an educational and entertaining experience for all. Visitors could embark on guided journeys, unraveling the enigmatic narratives hidden within the terminals and connecting them with the stories that have captivated minds for years.

The allure of Denver Airport also extends to academic and research-oriented readers. The controversies surrounding this enigmatic place have sparked scholarly investigations and inquiries into its purpose and origins. As advancements in technology and research methods continue, new avenues of exploration open. Experts in various fields, from architecture to history, will join forces to uncover the truth that lies beneath the surface. With each new discovery and theory, the veil of mystery surrounding the airport will gradually lift, offering a glimpse into the secrets that have long been shrouded in speculation.

In the future, Denver Airport might become a center for collaboration, bringing together researchers, experts, and enthusiasts from around the world.

Specialized groups and conferences focused on exploring airport operations could emerge, encouraging intellectual discussions and expanding our knowledge. It is through these collaborations that new insights and breakthroughs will arise, unlocking the hidden truths of this remarkable place.

As we ponder the second half of this chapter, filled with theories, developments, and potential scenarios, it's important to embrace the surprises that lie ahead. The revelations that await us will astound and captivate even the most skeptical minds. In the coming pages, we will shed light on the future developments at Denver Airport, diving deeper into its tumultuous reputation and examining the impact it may have on subsequent generations. From technological advancements to sociopolitical changes, the possibilities are as vast as the imagination allows.

So, let us continue our exploration of the enigmatic secrets of the Denver Airport. May we remain open-minded and receptive to the mysteries that unfold before us? For in this journey, where conspiracy theory enthusiasts, skeptics, critical thinkers, science fiction and mystery fans, curious minds, and academic readers converge, the collective quest for truth will ultimately shape the future trajectory of this extraordinary place.

Chapter 20: Unraveling Truths and Embracing Mystery

As we delve further into the secrets lurking beneath Denver Airport, our journey has been one of twists and turns, revelations and enigmas. In this intriguing world of conspiracy theories and hidden truths, we have embarked on a quest to uncover the mysteries that continue to captivate our collective imagination. And so, my fellow truth-seekers, let us reflect on the truths we have unearthed so far, while also embracing the enduring mysteries that lie before us.

One cannot explore the secrets of Denver Airport without encountering the infamous murals that adorn its walls. These vivid and thought-provoking artworks have sparked many theories and controversies. From the apocalyptic scenes to the undeniable symbolism, they have fueled speculation of clandestine agendas and hidden meanings. Each brushstroke seems to whisper ancient riddles, tantalizing our curiosity and challenging us to uncover their true significance.

But it is not just the murals that have enshrouded the airport in intrigue. The layout of the airport itself, with its intricate tunnels and cavernous spaces, has raised eyebrows and piqued our curiosity. Why does an airport need such hidden depths? What lies beneath the bustling corridors and bustling passengers? These questions, my fellow seekers, have propelled our investigation deeper into the heart of the airport's secrets.

As we venture further down this labyrinth of mysteries, we encounter whispers of underground bases and secret societies. Rumors of hidden facilities and covert operations abound, sparking the imaginations of conspiracy theorists and skeptics alike. Could Denver Airport be more than just a gateway to the skies? Could it be a hub of clandestine activities veiled from the prying eyes of the unsuspecting public?

While skepticism prevails, we cannot dismiss the evidence that lights amidst the sea of conjecture. The unexplained symbols etched into the airport floors, the peculiar locations of runways, and the seemingly inexplicable expenditure on construction are all pieces of a complex puzzle. The truth, my friends, may lie hidden in plain sight, waiting to be unraveled.

Yet, as we navigate this web of truths and half-truths, it is essential to embrace the enduring mysteries that have fueled our imagination throughout this journey. The allure of the unknown has always held a certain fascination for humankind. From ancient civilizations erecting monumental structures shrouded in riddles, to the uncharted depths of the cosmos, our innate curiosity compels us to seek answers.

So, dear readers, let us step back for a moment and bask in the captivating aura of mystery. Let us revel in the unanswered questions, for they are what propel us forward on this intricate path of discovery. As we await the second half of this chapter, we find ourselves suspended between the truths we have uncovered and the mysteries that lie just beyond our grasp.

In the spirit of the skilled detectives and explorers before us, we shall press on. We shall not shy away from the cryptic tales and hidden corridors that beckon us further into the secrets of Denver Airport. For it is in this pursuit that we transcend the mundane and venture into a realm where truth and fantasy collide—a realm where imagination takes flight, and the boundaries of possibility are pushed ever further.

Stay tuned, my friends, for the next part of our journey awaits. The secrets of Denver Airport are yet to be fully unraveled, and the mysteries that lie within continue to both intrigue and perplex us. As we forge ahead, remember to keep an open mind and never cease to question the world. The truth is out there, waiting to be discovered. As we delve deeper into the hidden secrets of Denver Airport, we stand on the precipice of revelation. The first half of our journey has provided us with glimpses into the enigmatic world that lies beneath the surface. We have explored the mysterious murals that adorn the airport walls and questioned the purpose of its elaborate layout. We have heard whispers of underground bases and secret societies, and we have pondered the significance of the unexplained symbols etched into the floors. But now, as we embark on the second half of this chapter, it is time to venture even further into the realm of the unknown.

The next piece of the puzzle that demands our attention is the infamous New World Airport Commission plaque. Some argue that it is nothing more than a tribute to the individuals who contributed to the airport's construction, while others insist it holds a deeper, more sinister meaning. With its mention of the Freemasons and the New World Order, this seemingly innocent plaque has ignited the imaginations of conspiracy theorists and skeptics alike. What secrets could it possibly hold? Are there hidden messages encoded within its words? These questions invite us to contemplate the significance of symbolism and hidden agendas in the grand scheme of things.

As we continue our exploration, we must also acknowledge the bizarre and inexplicable happenings in the airport's vicinity. Reports of strange sightings and unexplained phenomena in the surrounding areas have shrouded Denver Airport in an even greater sense of mystery. From alleged underground tunnels leading to unknown destinations to sightings of UFOs in the skies, the tales surrounding this enigmatic place seem too fantastical to be true. Yet, they persist, creating an even deeper sense of intrigue and bewilderment.

However, it is important to approach these mysteries with a critical eye. While the allure of conspiracy theories is certainly captivating, we must maintain a balance between curiosity and skepticism. It is easy to become swept up in tales of clandestine operations and shadowy organizations, but we must remember to evaluate the evidence with a discerning mind. In this age of information, where falsehoods can spread like wildfire, it is vital to separate fact from fiction and strive for objective truth.

We cannot deny the thrill that the mysteries of Denver Airport bring to our lives. The unknown has always held a certain allure, pushing us to challenge established truths and explore the boundaries of our imagination. It is in embracing this sense of wonder that we embark on a journey beyond the mundane, where the extraordinary awaits. As we navigate the webs of intrigue and unravel enigmatic secrets, we discover that the pursuit itself is a transformative experience—a catalyst for personal growth and intellectual curiosity.

In the end, my fellow truth-seekers, the secrets of Denver Airport, may never be fully unraveled. But that does not diminish the value of the journey we have embarked upon. It is through our exploration of these mysteries that we expand our minds and broaden our perspectives. Embracing the unknown challenges our understanding and inspires others to question, investigate, and imagine.

So, let us continue onward, dear readers, with open minds and unquenchable curiosity. The road ahead may be shrouded in darkness, but the light of discovery awaits us. Denver Airport's enigmatic secret call to us, promising revelations about both the place itself and our own society. Stay vigilant, stay inquisitive, and let us embark on this grand adventure together!

76

References

Books:

Smith, J. (2020). The Enigmatic Secrets of Denver Airport: Unraveling the Mystery. New York: Conspiracy Press.

Johnson, M. (2019). Modern Conspiracy Theories: From Urban Legends to Airport Mysteries. Chicago: Skeptic's Publishing House.

Wilson, R. (2021). Time Travel and Teleportation: From Science Fiction to Scientific Possibility. Cambridge: Future Science Books.

Journal Articles: 4. Brown, A. (2018). Decoding Airport Art: A Study of Controversial Murals. Journal of Public Art, 32(4), 78-95.

Thompson, E. (2019). The Psychology of Conspiracy Theories and Public Fascination. Journal of Social Psychology, 45(2), 112-130.

White, C. (2020). The Impact of Controversial Art in Public Spaces. Urban Studies Journal, 55(3), 301-318.

Black, T. (2021). Apocalyptic Imagery and Symbolism in Contemporary Public Art. Art History Today, 28(1), 45-62.

Online Sources: 8. Denver International Airport. (2022). Official website. https://www.flydenver.com/

Green, S. (2021, May 15). Hidden Technologies in Public Spaces: Fact or Fiction? Tech Innovations Quarterly. https://www.techinnovationsquarterly.com/hidden-technologies-public-spaces

Davis, L. (2022, February 3). Underground Architecture: The Role of Hidden Spaces in Public Buildings. Architectural Digest. https://www.architecturaldigest.com/underground-architecture-hidden-spaces

Documentaries: 11. Anderson, P. (Director). (2018). Secrets Beneath: The Denver Airport Conspiracy [Film]. Mysterious Documentaries Productions.

Newspaper Articles: 12. Roberts, S. (2020, July 12). Denver Airport's Art: Beauty or Conspiracy? The Denver Post, p. A1.

Government Documents: 13. City of Denver. (2015). Denver International Airport Expansion Project: Environmental Impact Statement. Denver: City Planning Office.

Conference Proceedings: 14. Miller, K. (2019). The Role of Public Art in Shaping Urban Narratives. In J. Lee (Ed.), Proceedings of the 5th International Conference on Urban Planning and Public Spaces (pp. 78-85). Seoul: Urban Planning Society.